PF
STOP T
BOARD BLAME GAME

MW01003972

"Hardy Smith has the credibility to write *Stop the Nonprofit Board Blame Game* as a tool to address the concerns of tens of thousands of nonprofit boards. This exciting new book offers real-world situations. Answers are provided based on extensive research, years of consultation, and the citations of respected business authors and leaders. A must-read for nominating committees to draw the best volunteer candidates."

—BOB HARRIS, CAE, NonprofitCenter.com

"I really like the use of personal stories along with the depth and diversity of other sources—not just nonprofit or fundraising sources—that make this book very, very cool! The included surveys and interviews are great and supported with lots of good examples, tips, and resources."

—SIMONE P. JOYAUX, ACFRE, Adv Dip, FAFP, author of *Keep Your Donors*, *Strategic Fund Development*, and *Firing Lousy Board Members*

"In the 30-plus years I've worked with nonprofits, board performance and engagement have always been a challenge. Hardy's strategies, helpful anecdotes, and sound recommendations will help strengthen the effectiveness of your board."

—ALYCE LEE STANSBURY, CFRE, founder/president, Stansbury Consulting

"Hardy Smith has compiled the most complete work on how to recruit, reward, and retain a high-performing nonprofit board that I have ever read. Don't put it on a shelf; keep it on your desk as a guide!"

—BARRY BANTHER, chairman of the board, National Speakers Association, former chairman of the board, Florida State Board of Independent Colleges and Universities

"Hardy's book, *Stop the Nonprofit Board Blame Game*, is every organization's 'must-have handbook' for developing the right board that goes beyond the current status quo. Engaging, informative, and solution oriented, this book should be included in your organization's handout to all board members. As a board member, you will learn the techniques and strategies that will allow you to hit the ground running and increase your nonprofit's performance, giving you a sense of pride for a job well done."

—CANDACE LIGHTNER, founder of Mothers Against Drunk Driving and We Save Lives

"Hardy Smith has successfully taken on the complex challenge of nonprofit board engagement. *Stop the Nonprofit Board Blame Game* identifies causes that contribute to board members not meeting expectations and provides solid action strategies to overcome those issues."

—NICK CRAW, former director, Peace Corps

"Hardy offers an in-depth look at board dynamics and practical ways to get staff and the board operating in a positive and productive manner. A must-read for nonprofit organizations."

—FRANK RUDD, CAE, CMP, president and CEO,
Florida Society of Association Executives

"In his personally researched book, *Stop the Nonprofit Board Blame Game*, Hardy Smith identifies tangible and time-tested processes that go a long way toward improving the effectiveness, rewards, and meaningful outcomes from leaders serving on boards of directors."

—TIM JACKSON, CMP, CAE, president/CEO,
Colorado Automobile Dealers Association

"Hardy Smith's new book on boards, including chamber boards, is a must-read for all chamber CEOs, board chairs, and board members. The wisdom and words of advice contained in the pages will greatly improve your organization, when implemented."

—FRANK J. KENNY, founder, Chamber Pros Community

"Positive, productive relationships between board members and staff are the key to success for nonprofit boards. In this blueprint, Hardy Smith provides tips for avoiding relationship mistakes that contribute to board member disengagement."

—RUBY NEWELL-LEGNER, fan experience expert at 7 Star Service,
past president, National Speakers Association

"Most board books are written from the organization's perspective. Hardy has flipped the script and highlights volunteers' voices, offering a unique approach to stopping the blame game."

—MARY BYERS, CAE, CSP, author of *Race for Relevance:*
5 Radical Changes for Associations

"This is the book we've needed. Hardy provides a fresh perspective on the challenges faced by nonprofit boards. He provides lighthearted but meaningful analogies combined with practical solutions. The guided questions in each chapter allow nonprofit leaders to make real action plans that will lead to positive changes for their organizations."

—SARA LEONARD, MBA, CFR, Sara Leonard Group

STOP

THE NONPROFIT BOARD

BLAME

GAME

How to Break the Cycle of Frustrating Relationships
and Benefit from Fully Engaged Boards

HARDY SMITH

RIVER GROVE
BOOKS

Published by River Grove Books
Austin, TX
www.rivergrovebooks.com

Distributed by River Grove Books

Design and composition by Greenleaf Book Group
Cover design by Greenleaf Book Group
Edited by Denise McCabe | McCabe Editing | McCabeediting.com

Grateful acknowledgment is made to the following sources for permission to reproduce copyrighted material.
American Society of Association Executives (ASAE). Call to Fill Officer and Board Vacancies. Copyright © by the American Society of Association Executives. All Rights Reserved. Reproduced by permission.
Florida Society of Association Executives (FSAE). Call for Board Nominations. Copyright © the Florida Society of Association Executives. All Rights Reserved. Reproduced by permission.
National Speakers Association (NSA). Call for Board Nominations. Copyright © by the National Speakers Association. All Rights Reserved. Reproduced by permission.
Quantum Leap Systems. Various materials. Copyright © 1999, 2021 Quantum Leap Systems, Inc. All Rights Reserved. Reproduced by permission.

Publisher's Cataloging-in-Publication data is available.

Print ISBN: 978-1-63299-480-6

eBook ISBN: 978-1-63299-481-3

First Edition

CONTENTS

FOREWORD

Let a pro guide you through board challenges and solutions. Hardy Smith has the credibility to write *Stop the Nonprofit Board Blame Game* as a tool to address the concerns of tens of thousands of nonprofit boards.

He has seen and heard the highs and lows of board members and their achievements and failures. He's listened to the plaints of executive directors who ask, "Why won't the directors do what they should to achieve our organization's mission and strategic goals?"

This exciting new book offers real world situations. Answers are provided based on extensive research, years of consultation, and the citations of respected business authors and leaders.

Hardy adds value by addressing two perspectives. Read this book through the eyes of the volunteer directors, and with the concerns of exasperated executive directors in mind. The chapters take readers from volunteer selection and on-boarding to strategic thinking and understanding governance roles.

Through all his wisdom I am reminded of the most important adage in every nonprofit: "The board governs, and the staff manage." Together they form a partnership.

Hardy is straightforward about addressing governance frustrations and dysfunctions and offers a wealth of tips and examples. This is a book to lay on every boardroom table. It is a must-read for nominating committees to draw the best volunteer candidates.

BOB HARRIS, CAE

www.nonprofitcenter.com

INTRODUCTION

You're walking on the beach, deep in thought on how you can get your board to do what it's supposed to do, and you see that a big wave has just deposited a barnacle-covered bottle. You open the top, and out pops a genie who says, "Thank you for freeing me! To reward you, I will give you one wish."

You immediately know how you will take advantage of this most amazing opportunity. You excitedly respond, "My wish would be to have a perfect board for the nonprofit I work with—a board that is engaged, works collaboratively, fulfills its expected performance obligations, and provides positive, productive guidance!"

"Your wish is granted," says the genie.

Now wouldn't that be nice, to find a genie who would make that perfect board wish happen? Not exactly reality, is it? What is real is that there is a lot of frustration associated with nonprofit boards. Both staff and board members are frustrated and want solutions that will fix the challenges.

If you are a nonprofit or association professional who is frustrated with boards and board members who are not living up to expectations, this book has been written with *you* in mind. Likewise, if you are a volunteer board member who has experienced a less than satisfactory board service experience, this book has been written with *you* in mind.

This book-writing journey was triggered by my curiosity about the negativity often associated with board member performance. To develop a pool of experienced board members willing to help with this project, I reached out to my nationwide network developed over more than four decades of personal and professional involvement with nonprofit, volunteer, and membership-based organizations. The respondents to my request for feedback represent what could be considered a blue-chip list of board members from across the country. They include business and community leaders who serve as board members of nonprofits, associations, and community organizations. The respondents reflect a wide variety of occupations and interests, including university presidents, top corporate executives, business owners, association CEOs, retirees, teachers, community activists, political leaders, attorneys, engineers, management and nonmanagement-level employees, a college basketball official, and dedicated volunteers.

I will admit my survey methodology was not that of a professional researcher. As it turned out, though, I believe my approach generated eye-opening results that otherwise would not have been possible. Using open-ended questions allowed for responses that were very revealing. As the comments came in, a commonality emerged: Despite geographic and demographic differences, in addition to varying levels of experience, the collective response indicated a focused list of issues that contribute to members not meeting their board performance expectations.

To my surprise, a totally unexpected revelation surfaced. The survey participants candidly expressed that they, too, often experience frustration with their time spent in board service. These feelings proved to be a strong common denominator among the group, and there were many shared opinions on the causes of their dissatisfaction, as well as some divergence.

So, news flash to nonprofit leaders: Those board members you're frustrated with are quite possibly frustrated with you, too. Furthermore, the frustration felt by board members is a major reason that good performers become disengaged.

There are plenty of opinions available to boards about how they should be performing. In addition, while board performance is certainly a frequently discussed problem, the most commonly suggested solutions—especially training—don't appear to be working. It's difficult to instruct someone to stop being unhappy. I am convinced that ending the frustration with nonprofit boards requires an alternative approach.

This book is based on the board members' perspective. It offers their opinions and feelings about board service, which they are passionate about. I have learned that you can't argue with someone about their feelings, so it's important to take what's shared at face value and learn from it.

This book is about the why in *Why don't board members do what they're supposed to do?* But I wanted to go beyond the why, beyond merely identifying issues; to that end, I have detailed many workable strategies with plenty of action steps. These solutions are based on suggestions from the board members and from my own experience, and they are supplemented with highly respected resources willing to share their expertise.

My research indicates that there are frequently repeated mistakes affecting relationships between nonprofit organizations and their board members. There are also continuously recurring errors that set organizations up for board performance failure. Clearly, stopping the cycle of repeated blunders—both those identified by the board members participating in my survey and those that I have observed—will eliminate many of the causes of frustration. Whether you are a staff professional or a volunteer board member experiencing frustration, you are, unfortunately, not alone.

This frustration, shared by so many, manifests in a variety of ways. One of the most prevalent is dysfunctional relationships, both between the organization and its board members and among board members themselves. Anyone who has undergone relationship counseling becomes aware that commitment from both parties is needed to make the relationship work. Addressing the issues at hand and working together for resolution is the path to relationship success. The same corrective course will improve board relationships. Collaboratively taking action to make needed repairs will create a platform for correcting practices that have led to a breakdown in board performance.

My intention in writing this book is to create a practical resource that provides guidance for implementing these corrective actions. I identify four difference-making concepts that will stop frustration with nonprofit boards.

First, we must break the cycle of dysfunctional board relationships. Change in the approach to board engagement is needed. I urge organizations to pay attention to the board member perspective, which is too often not considered.

We must then find the right people; a mismatch between people and the board they serve on is often a source of board-related frustration. Good people with good intentions don't automatically make good board members. Recurring recruitment mistakes predictably doom a board to unfulfilled potential.

I provide practical how-tos for avoiding those mistakes relating to board member selection.

Next, we must create a positive board experience. When good, productive board members have a not-so-good experience, they become disengaged. However, when the experience is positive and rewarding, the results can be dynamic. I identify action priorities that are essential elements for solid relationships. Committing to the recommended techniques for relationship building will make a significant difference in board engagement.

Finally, we must adapt to meet new challenges that will influence the organization's ability to successfully achieve its mission. Developing boards as high-value assets will give nonprofits a stronger platform for overcoming the issues ahead and taking advantage of future opportunities. I provide action steps focused on how to strengthen boards, so they are best able to meet leadership and performance expectations.

If you are part of an organization staff and use this book as a resource, you will benefit from the board member perspective. If you are a board member, you will recognize issues you have observed or encountered. You will also see how to help boards you are a member of meet their expectations.

Thank you to the many dedicated board members who took the time to share the benefit of your board service insights. Your frank observations on board service issues and solutions for positive and productive relationships will provide invaluable guidance to those who share your passion for doing good.

Break the Cycle of Dysfunctional Board Relationships

1

REVIEW SURPRISING SURVEY RESULTS

"**W**hat is your number-one problem?" I ask a roomful of non-profit leaders.

They are, for the most part, shocked at their collective response to a workshop leader's simple question focusing on their perspective. The replies are loud, forceful, and nearly in unison:

"It's those board members! Why don't they do what they're supposed to do?"

An excited buzz fills the room following the group's dramatic and spontaneous reaction. I follow up with three additional questions:

- Do the board members whose performance is being criticized know what your expectation is?

- If so, how is that being communicated?

- Are you asking them, or are you telling them?

The silence that follows is equally as dramatic as the group's initial reaction. The second shocker to hit these nonprofit leaders is that their own actions could be contributing to the problem they identify as their major distress.

The exchange, triggered during this exercise in self-discovery for them, creates a significant aha! moment for me.

The level of energy in which the audience responses are delivered indicates the obvious existence of two major problems that nonprofits and other organizations relying on volunteer leadership are experiencing: The organizations aren't getting what they expect from their boards, and they have failed to adequately communicate their expectations. The surprise is that everyone recognizes the first problem, but they have not addressed it.

The criticism of board member performance is certainly not new, but current approaches to correct performance failures don't seem to be working; too many organizations continue to voice intense frustration with their board members. Further evidence of that frustration can be seen in the number of books and publications, workshops, and social media discussions that deal with the topic of board performance. My own social media posts on board performance always generate a lively response.

> **The criticism of board member performance is certainly not new, but current approaches to correct performance failures don't seem to be working.**

Identifying how important these issues are—and the critical links between them—prompted me to undertake my first objective: to discover the whys in the question *Why don't board members do what they're supposed to do?* The answers were in the survey responses.

After gaining an understanding of

board member perspective relative to nonprofit participation, I formulated my second objective: to identify reasonable and doable actions to help nonprofits, associations, volunteer- and member-based organizations, and community groups ensure that their board members function for the good of their mission.

As a starting point, I solicited input from board members with a survey of these five questions:

- What is your biggest criticism related to organizations and their relationships with their boards?

- Why don't board members do what they're supposed to do?

- When asked to serve on a nonprofit board, what prompts you to say no?

- When asked to serve on a nonprofit board, what motivates you to say yes?

- How can an organization be more effective in using its board members?

The questions allowed for open-ended responses that would reflect the individual's thoughts, feelings, and personal board member experiences.

When creating and analyzing the collection of replies, I realized that this project would be unique among efforts to address board member performance. The traditional approach seems to focus on telling board members and the organizations they serve that there is a certain behavior template that should be adhered to.

Attempts to correct underperforming boards seem to include a lot of one-way communication.

My approach was to listen to experienced board members and share their collective advice for improving the performance of any board member. The participants in the survey, it turns out, were happy to be asked for—instead of told—their perspectives. They were eager to share their experiences and their suggestions for improvement.

The combination of asking and really listening led to the action steps that give organizations the advantage of knowing what's been missing from their dialogue on board performance: the valuable voice of the board members themselves.

I found two common stances among the survey participants. First, they have a strong passion for their volunteer involvement. Doesn't this strike you as interesting, since, as a group, their performance attracts such uniform criticism? Second, they have a great deal of frustration with that volunteer involvement. Doesn't this, too, strike you as ironic, given that criticism? The communication necessary to fix both the staffs' criticism and the boards' frustration is missing.

In the chapters ahead, through the insights from this board member focus group, we will identify behaviors and their causes that create anxiety for organizations and board members alike. Only by understanding the causes can solutions be identified and executed. We will challenge longtime beliefs and practices on the part of both nonprofits and their boards that reinforce a continuing cycle of mistakes and the perpetuation of unrealistic expectations.

....

Develop your action steps

- Have you ever felt frustration with your board?

- Are you aware of issues that may contribute to board members not performing as expected?

- What actions can you take to discover how your board members feel about their board experience?

2

ACKNOWLEDGE WHY
CHANGE IS NEEDED

A group of like-minded individuals recognizing a significant problem in their community agreed to organize a nonprofit to address it. With good intentions, they eagerly set about doing the good work of their stated mission. Unfortunately, they ignored the recommendation of working with a solid business plan because they saw taking time to plan as a distraction from the work they were busy doing. After several years of success, a few of the founding board members moved on to other interests. Recruiting new board members with the same passion as the founders had not been a priority. The board, whose members no longer had a shared vision of the mission, became embroiled in disagreements over what direction to take. This board dysfunction led to staff resignations. Then, during a downturn in the economy, the nonprofit's main sponsor withdrew support.

Trying to navigate without the benefit of good planning, which would have allowed the nonprofit's leadership team to anticipate, minimize, or even avoid potential problems, proved to be a big mistake. Without positive, cohesive leadership, the nonprofit began to flounder and eventually closed its doors. The shutdown meant those who came to depend on the services that had been provided were now without help.

How sad would this story be if it were about your nonprofit? Thousands of nonprofits go by the wayside every year. A desire to do good does not guarantee success forever. Organizations unprepared to deal with the ever-changing influences that can affect their ability to achieve their mission put themselves and the cause they serve at risk.

The increasingly complicated challenges facing nonprofits and associations are making it more difficult for them to achieve their missions. Indeed, for many, the challenges threaten their very existence. Let's look at some of the perils now confronting the business of doing good. Just for starters: Declining membership, poor donor retention rates, escalating demands for services, a revolving door of volunteers, and a growing competition for a shrinking pool of available resources are all contributing to a buildup of tremendous pressure on the foundations supporting nonprofits and associations.

The challenges don't end there. A major exodus from senior staff positions is occurring as a generation of dedicated professionals with longtime experience has reached retirement age. Compounding this loss of institutional knowledge are reports indicating that many in the pool of potential nonprofit sector next-gen leaders aren't interested in advancing to top leadership roles. They see the stress and the pressure and are not motivated to subject themselves to that environment.

The nation's population is undergoing rapid transformation. Our demographics today are dramatically different from our makeup just a few short decades ago. As the trend continues, cultural and generational differences will greatly influence how future volunteers, donors, board members, and professional staff—not to mention those who benefit from the services they provide—think and act. It is a generational shift.

Five distinctly different generations now make up our national demographic. They are seniors (born 1922–1945), baby boomers (born 1946–1964), Generation X (born 1965–1980), Generation Y (born 1981–2001), and Generation Z (born 2001–2011).

Please note this caveat: The birth ranges are approximations, and individuals can have personality traits that overlap those of other generational groups. Don't automatically assume what someone's opinion may be or predict behavior based solely on their birth date.

Organizations are well advised to invest time in understanding the diverse characteristics represented by each group. Recognizing the personal preferences they identify with is key to establishing positive, long-lasting relationships.

There is another significant trend that organizations must take into account. The phenomenon of social disengagement is creating a dramatic effect and further adds to the conflict and challenges faced by organizations. Groups that seek social engagement to advance a cause, as well as those that are dependent on volunteers or members, are well aware of this ongoing decline.

According to Robert Putnam, in his book *Bowling Alone*, we are, indeed, becoming a disengaged society. My observations in the years since confirm that this disengagement continues. Putnam is a political scientist and a professor of public policy at Harvard. His book is considered the definitive work on volunteer and membership disengagement in this country. It's an intriguing statistical analysis. If your organization depends on volunteers or members, this book is a must read. Putnam's historical review of participation data reports that, after a buildup that began in the late 1890s, the trend toward a reversal in social and organizational participation started in the 1960s. Volunteerism, membership engagement, and social involvement in this country began a downward spiral that continues today and shows no sign of recovery.

Although there are a few exceptions, most types of similar groups—such as political parties, school support auxiliaries, trade unions, the Boy Scouts, the Girl Scouts, charitable groups like United Way, professional associations, churches, and chambers of commerce—are affected.

This means that, in general, we are becoming less interested in in-person interaction with each other. We have evolved (devolved?) from shaking hands at church socials and barn raisings to using touch screens to surf the Internet and social media. In addition, nonprofits and associations are facing more intense accountability from external quarters. They are feeling the pressure of greater scrutiny by government regulators and the media. Donors are also becoming more discerning and are asking more questions associated with oversight before committing their financial support. And governance is playing a more significant role for board members than ever before.

For example, in the past, some organizations have recruited board members by telling them not to worry about being actively involved in board work. Everyone was satisfied with just having the nonparticipating board members lending their name to a letterhead, making a sizable contribution, or just helping with fundraising. Today, higher standards of governance compliance require attention to fiduciary responsibility, accountability, liability, and transparency. Board members are finding out they could be personally liable for those meetings they didn't attend, those minutes they didn't read, and those financial statements they approved without questioning.

All of these factors influence the decisions of those considering whether to accept or continue holding a board position. This means getting and keeping the board members your organization needs will rise to a greater degree of difficulty. A prospective board member may think, *Being on a nonprofit board used to be a lot of fun. We had some nice dinners and played golf once a year. Now, this is like a job.* And they would be absolutely right.

ARE NONPROFITS HEEDING WARNINGS?

While there certainly are organizations taking proactive measures to address these issues, many are not. Some claim they're too busy. Some declare they don't have the resources to invest in the help they need. Some believe that, as long as they are doing obvious good, they don't have to worry about their future. Some just don't have the leadership in place to bring about necessary change.

All of these excuses bring to mind the story of the man who chose to ignore warnings of an impending flood and turned down offers for help. With ominous clouds covering the morning sky, the weather forecast warned that an already rain-swollen river might threaten the dam that kept the town safe from flooding. The indifferent man paid no attention. Even when the dam showed signs of giving way and the town leaders called for immediate evacuation, the man asked, "Even if it floods, how bad can it be?"

Even if it floods, how bad can it be?

Finally, unable to hold back the rising river any longer, the dam broke. A rescue team attempted to save the man from the roof of his house, but he declared, "The rain will stop soon, and the water will go down." As the water continued to rise and swept him away, the man looked to the sky and angrily yelled, "Why didn't you save me?"

Before going under for the final time, he heard a stern reply, "You had the weather report. You were told to evacuate. The rescue team came for you. You had your chances to be saved."

This age-old tale illustrates a timeless lesson: When the environment changes, ignoring challenges is not a strategy that will keep you safe. Understanding how important issues impact board dynamics—and vice versa—can determine survival. If a competent board represents a life jacket for an organization, don't be among the many that realize they don't have life-saving equipment onboard.

If used properly, boards can be a positive asset for leading an organization through difficult circumstances. The right board members—from the newest members to the most seasoned leadership—who bring dedication to a cause can be the source of ideas and resources that ensures the organization's future.

....

Develop your action steps

- What change is affecting your nonprofit?

- How does this change affect your board?

- How are you involving your board to address these challenges?

3

LISTEN TO YOUR
BOARD MEMBERS

The opinions that board members voice about their volunteer service spring from passionate dedication, and what they have to say is quite revealing. Organizations and board leaders alike can benefit from paying close attention to what our survey participants have been willing to share: observations and advice regarding some of the most challenging board engagement issues faced by nonprofits.

The participants' willingness to answer questions and elaborate on their board experiences yields candid feedback that sets the stage for deeper examination. Later, we will delve into these topics and provide specific solutions to perplexing board performance problems. The critiques that the board members offer are not meant to be negative. These board members volunteer and serve causes because they want to make a positive difference. Their participation in this project was in the spirit of helping to correct situations that impede the ability of organizations with important missions to reach their full potential.

It's important to note that the responses are not the isolated reactions of perhaps a disgruntled board member or two that can be easily dismissed. Although they present a varied range of perspectives, they also demonstrate a strong common focus on the welfare of the organization and its board members and on their relationships. The feedback is the core message of this work.

Here are the participants in their own words.

WHAT IS YOUR BIGGEST CRITICISM RELATED TO ORGANIZATIONS AND THEIR RELATIONSHIPS WITH THEIR BOARDS?

Asking board members for their biggest criticism related to boards and the organizations they serve opened the floodgates. Their responses fall into seven categories: communication, expecting too much, conflict with staff, conflict within the board, wasted time, a lack of organization, and the wrong people.

Communication

The key contributor to board member disengagement is poor communication. When asked for examples of communication fails, our board members have plenty to say.

Riverside, Alabama, mayor Rusty Jessup is adamant about the importance of communication: "A lack of communication about expected performance is my biggest criticism. I also believe that openness about differences when they exist is essential. Don't pretend there is not a problem. Never ignore the 1,000-pound gorilla in the corner. Don't sugarcoat anything for PR purposes. Close your meeting to the public if necessary, but talk about the gorilla."

"I don't want surprises—especially the bad type," states Ron Nowviskie, who has been a dedicated board member to numerous organizations. "Give me complex information well in advance of meetings so I can adequately review it."

Bossier City, Louisiana, mayor Don Jones says it's an issue for him "when staff controls how much volunteer board members know."

Financial advisor John Lowery laments the "lack of details or necessary information on an ongoing basis. Too many nonprofits expect a rubber stamp board and don't keep the board fully informed."

Respected volunteer leader Lamar Smith targets executive directors. "Some executive directors just don't seem to communicate enough information. They should do a better job with websites, newsletters, and personal notes."

Dedicated community volunteer Kim Newlin, carrying the personal touch a step further, doesn't appreciate the "lack of personal communication—with all interaction done by letter or email, with little or no personal contact."

"I have been on both sides of this one," shares Jim McCarthy, who has extensive volunteer board experience. "The staff needs to understand that most board members do not think about the board until they are on the way to a meeting. They need a friendly reminder on what they have committed to do. Short deadlines and accountability to other board members work well. Generally speaking, good follow-up communication won't happen unless the staff makes it happen."

Of course, communication goes both ways.

Hospitality industry leader Bob Davis advocates, "Get board members involved in the process, ask their opinions, get them to buy in. Don't just hand them an agenda."

Community cause supporter Mary Thomas advises, "Communicate to the board what it is that you want from them and allow their input on what it is they can contribute or not contribute in support."

For chamber of commerce staff member Mary Boggs, good communication means involvement. "Everyone wants to not only feel needed but to also be a part of the process."

From his perspective, longtime board service member David Serota puts a fine point on it. "Communication is a two-way street, and both staff and board members must work diligently to ensure that timely and accurate communication occurs at all times."

Expecting too much

An extension of communication issues is the problem of expecting too much. Board members can feel blindsided by assumptions.

Super mom volunteer Lori Tolland feels strongly about this. "My biggest criticism is the lack of communication of expectations."

And community leader Mary Swiderski goes further. "I believe staff expects too much from their boards."

Business owner John Koberg doesn't want to serve on a board where there is "too much reliance on too few board members."

Community champion Brad Giles believes that "boards attempt too much during a single year. They gain more involvement from board members if they focus on fewer projects with larger impacts."

And board member Anthony Ziner sees it as a deal breaker when "there's an expectation that you will serve as an ancillary workforce and be tasked with doing things that are the province of paid staff."

Also critical of time demands is T. K. Wetherell, former

president of Florida State University and former speaker of the Florida House of Representatives. "Organizations often expect more and more of board members who have lives and businesses to run. Ask only when you need their help and limit the asks to something that can make a difference."

Conflicts with staff

A board of directors sets policy, and the staff executes it. The two groups complement each other and do so best when clarity minimizes conflict. When the staff doesn't recognize its role, a variety of problems can occur. Board members share several criticisms about staff-related issues that affect board relationships. Some are tough to hear.

"Staff sometimes has very passive-aggressive behavior. They don't ask for the help they want or need and then resent board members for not being involved," observes business journal publisher Joyce Hayhow.

Educator Kathy Fletcher's criticism is a lack of clarity of responsibilities: "not having clear definition of duties of where board responsibilities begin and end. Also, when the executive director is not a leader."

Engineer and manufacturing CEO Paul Clare cites problems that arise when conflicts and their causes are not addressed. "Some organizations fail to communicate with boards in a give-and-take setting on a regular basis. These meetings can be informal or formal. Some organizations do not require their boards to evaluate themselves and their relationship with the organization. In some cases, boards are not large enough to spread the workload, thus putting too much work on too few."

Ladies Professional Golf Association executive Carol Kilian sees staff and board not being aligned as a source of relationship problems. "Often, the vision of the board members does not coincide with the organization's chief executive officer, who has to deal with operational functions on a daily basis. It's hard to marry the two when one is planning oriented, and the other is function oriented. The two should be able to help each other so positive plans and solutions can be discussed and delivered. One side should not work independently of the other, and I have found that often occurs."

Passionate board member Iris Bly sees a red flag "when people are afraid to speak up and worry about what others might think." Organizations should ensure board members feel safe in expressing their thoughts.

Conflict within the board

Internal conflict comes in for a good dose of criticism. It's hard to be productive when there are negative relationships in the boardroom.

Internationally involved volunteer leader Bob Lindholm sees conflict naturally occur when "a chairman or organization shows disregard for the board's advice."

Association CEO Wilson Wright cites two frustrations: "when the leadership won't give me the tools or authority to get my assignment done and when ideas of newcomers are rejected."

Utility company representative Phil Tornelli, too, has been a witness to this behavior. "Too many times, I have found that there are a few who dominate the meetings with very little input from the overall board."

Environmental activist Clay Henderson also sees the lack of inclusion as a point of conflict. "I start getting off boards when I see small groups of board members making all of the decisions between the meetings and then asking the full board to in effect ratify decisions after the fact."

Public relations pro Dotti Lewis shares, "I have turned down a reappointment because of frustration with a board that talked continuously but never took action."

Dave DeLaney, with a wide range of involvement, has experienced contention "when board members are too close to the operations of the organization, and they cannot make required decisions for the good of the group."

Kathy Schissler, a personal development coach, believes in the importance of constructive disagreement and that boards miss out when they avoid it. "Instead of having powerful conversations, people choose rather to be polite, safe, and right."

Wasted time

Board members are busy. They can be not only unhappy but, indeed, insulted when they feel their time is being wasted.

Transportation planner Gary Huttmann states, "I want my time to be productive."

Local advocate Sandy Geroux has seen the consequences of this challenge. "Make meetings productive. Too many meetings are held just to hold meetings and nothing ever gets done. This demotivates people."

Local government leader Suzanne Konchan has a problem when she sees "a weak board or one whose meetings are frustrating, contentious, or a waste of time."

In real estate executive Claire Hunter's opinion, the practice of wasting time simply shows "lack of respect for the board members' time. When staff or the executive director are not prepared or organized for board meetings, that is an issue."

This insight from Dr. Jack Hawkins, chancellor of Troy University, pulls things together. "Too often, valuable time is wasted via process. Opinion leaders are busy people and do not desire to waste their time in unproductive exercises. Plan focused meetings, and present professionally."

A lack of organization

Board members want organizations they serve to have a clear direction and to maintain their focus.

Julie Rand, with involvement in a number of organizations, looks unfavorably on "poorly run organizations, a lack of financial stability, and too much of a time commitment."

Banker Dave Timmons has seen problems arise "when meetings are too long or unstructured." Management consultant Paul Pendorf is particularly irked "when the chair doesn't know how to run a meeting according to Robert's Rules."

Corporate leader Bryan Sperber lists a "lack of thought about board members' expectations; also, poor execution of events, poor quality of meetings, and lack of interaction with other board members."

Hobbs, New Mexico, Chamber of Commerce president Ray Battaglini thinks about the future and how things may evolve "when mission or goals are unrealistic. Not having a leadership retreat or planning session and focusing on what needs to be done, and not providing the manpower and financial resources to make it happen."

Community leader icon Jay Adams ties it up with "the lack of a good solid plan."

The wrong people

Many board members agree that boards often underperform because they don't have the right people on them. How does this happen?

Educator Dr. Cay Davis knows it occurs "when people are asked to serve because of who they are, not because of what they can do."

Corporate president Phil Maroney has seen "20 percent do 80 percent of the work and board members selected for their company name versus what they can produce." He adds, "Failure to enforce attendance criteria" allows nonperformers to take board seats that could otherwise be filled with performers.

As insurance business CEO Charlie Lydecker notes, there is another risk when prospects are selected because they perform well on another board. "Select board members carefully. A person may be a great board member for one organization and a poor choice for another."

Accounting firm president Gary Lazetera cautions, "Don't allow people to take up space on a board without commitment."

Retail business owner Rose Ann Tornatore reinforces these views. "Not enough businesspeople, not enough participation, and when people are there in name only all mean you have the wrong people."

Obviously, some of the concerns raised in response to the first question will resurface with different applications in replies to the other four.

WHY DON'T BOARD MEMBERS DO WHAT THEY'RE SUPPOSED TO DO?

The survey respondents identified many reasons board members might not perform as staff desires. Their concerns fall into three categories: recruiting, leadership, and accountability.

More targeted recruiting

Marketing professional Mike Manning sets the theme. "Screen potential candidates better. Don't just take the first warm body."

Rhode Island's Arthur Plitt advises, "Decide what your organization does, and find the people to fit that direction."

This approach is shared by real estate agent Bonda Garrison. "Define the role, and recruit people who agree to fulfill that role."

Banker Mark Blanford likewise suggests, "Do a better job of evaluating potential board members. Make sure they are a good fit, and agree to do what is necessary for success." The important phrase from both respondents is "agree to."

Professional speaker Monica Wofford cites more recruiting specifics. "Be clear in what types of characteristics one is looking for in board members—high initiative, community connected, personal contributors of time only or of money as well."

Similarly, NCAA basketball official J. B. Caldwell's recommendation is to solicit and select "the right people who have the expertise and time that allow for expectations to be met."

Sarah Vandagriff, a real estate broker and commercial property manager, agrees with the focus on matching the person with the job. "Pick members who have contacts and talents that match the need. Make sure individuals have off-board relationships with each other, and they will work better together."

As a way to vet board prospects, experienced board leader Sam Willett advocates asking "for participation on committees before making them board members."

Based on his experience with recruiting, business owner and local fundraising master Kevin Bowler has this insight: "Too many people serve on the same boards, and that creates dilution."

NASCAR public relations veteran Kristy King offers this recruiting strategy: "When I actively go out searching for board members, I try not to go for the president or CEO of companies. The majority of time, they do not have the time to put in many hours, nor do they tend to roll up their sleeves and work side by side with folks."

Board reappointments should not be automatic, counsels lobbyist Sharon Crow. "Have a rotating board member expiration date with a list of criteria that need to be met to be reappointed."

Debbie Smith, who has extensive community involvement experience, has sound, forward-looking advice. "Get people who can make an impact. Keep the board fresh, and go after people with new ideas."

Leadership

Leadership shortcomings lead to board member failures. When leadership does not perform as it should, board members will not carry out duties as they should—and may not even be aware of them.

Aubrey Harris, experienced corporate marketing professional, sees problems arise from a "lack of leadership and direction."

Corporate executive Ed Williams believes that board performance is influenced by "possible gaps in communications or relationships between an organization's leadership and the board."

Andrew Gurtis, who has provided leadership to many charitable causes, explains, "Oftentimes, there is poor direction from the organization's leadership or staff as to board member responsibilities. Quantification of what's expected from a board member's time, treasure, and talents goes a long way in achieving effective board participation."

In nonprofit CEO Robin King's experience, quite often, board members aren't meeting expectations because they "weren't clearly advised of their responsibilities during an entrance interview (and many boards don't do them). Leadership establishing expectations and relationships before members join has always been very helpful to me to determine how much time will be required and what the expectations are."

Oklahoma volunteer leader Stan Moffat observes, "Usually, the task is not well defined, or there is no leadership that's making things happen. Organizations are only as good as the person at the top."

Corporate executive David Perryman reminds us that "board members don't wake up in the morning thinking about a particular nonprofit issue. They have their own businesses to think about. Staff must lead the board and use it as a resource to deal with issues."

Chamber of commerce CEO Barry Kennedy advises, "Make sure your board members get a good orientation on what is expected of them and continuous communications on the progress of the organization."

Accountability

Emphasis on accountability elevates board member performance.

"Some board members don't do what they are supposed to do because they don't feel accountability," says board president Greg Snell.

Attorney Mark Hall specifies a "lack of structure, direction, and accountability" to make the same point.

Community cause dynamo Bobbi Coleman is of the same opinion. "There's little accountability for board members. Too many board members like to come up with ideas and then want someone else to do it all," totally avoiding work commitment.

Board member Scott Jacobs suggests, "Make sure duties are clearly spelled out and action plans and accountability are in place."

Chamber of commerce CEO Greg Blose puts it vividly. "There needs to be some sort of accountability measures put in place that include verification and consequences of responsibility not done, so action is there for holding people's feet to the fire."

WHEN ASKED TO SERVE ON A NONPROFIT BOARD, WHAT PROMPTS YOU TO SAY NO?

When an organization receives repeated rejections from board prospects, it is a clarion call to determine the true reasons and the corrective action to be taken. Considerations that influenced the respondents to decline a board invitation fall into three categories: reputation, fundraising, and the perception of the organization's impact.

Reputation

Among other issues, a negative reputation is almost certain to result in no thank yous to board invites. Our respondents consider a wide range of issues.

The most serious concern comes from Jim McMahon, who is passionate about board service. "If there is a possibility of a board being sued for misconduct or [if that board] is known for misadventures, financial problems, or character issues by its members, that's a personal liability I don't want to be associated with."

Community volunteer Tony Bazile may decline an invitation depending on "other members of the board, ineffectiveness, and disorganization of the organization."

Corporate community representative John Poage adds to the list "those with a lack of credibility, unclear mission or duplication of effort, anything ethically questionable, or an impression that the board or organization is disorganized."

A board is unlikely to gain NASCAR public affairs director Cheryl Coxwell's membership "if the board's role is not clearly defined or its only purpose is to raise money, or if the reputation of the nonprofit is less than stellar."

Financial services professional Michael O'Connell sees a red flag when he has a "disagreement with the board's governance philosophy."

"I always give heavy consideration to the strength of the executive director and administration of the nonprofit," offers state representative Tom Leek. "If they are weak, I am more likely to say no."

Boards to be avoided are "boards that lack direction," shares board volunteer James Brown.

For school district leader Thomas Besaw, it's boards "with weak policies and procedures."

State championship basketball coach Charles Brinkerhoff responds with a no when "I doubt the value of the organization to the community or am concerned about the priorities of the organization."

Fundraising

Some of the respondents do not view direct solicitation fundraising by board members as a positive. If it's a requirement, it could be a deal breaker.

Marketing expert Dean O'Brien is turned off when "board members are expected to do fundraising."

With leadership in multiple community organizations, John Ferguson agrees. He declines "when the only purpose of the board is to ask people for money."

Hotelier Blaine Lansberry has served on many boards but is sure to reject an offer if she feels she is "being asked just so I'll contribute money."

Public relations agency owner Michael Jiloty identifies several fundraising concerns. "I often see a lack of sensitivity to the financial demands on board members, most of whom belong to several boards and get multiple requests for money. Certainly in need of more consideration is when the board member is personally making a contribution as opposed to when the individual's company is paying."

Rafael Ramirez has served on numerous boards and wants leadership to tell him in advance if he's being invited to join for the usual reason. He advises against making a seat on the board revolve around fundraising. "Often, these positions are only about fundraising, and after serving on many boards, it gets old having to call on the same people all the time."

North Carolina's David Haxton relates that he "declined a board position for an organization that I have been a donor to for more than twenty years because it involved fundraising."

Perception of impact

Performance-minded individuals who want to invest their time in activities that make a difference won't get involved if they feel their efforts will be fruitless.

University professor Jim Cunningham says no when "the board's decision-making powers are so limited that the members seem to be figureheads and not contributing members of leadership. I've been on those boards, and they are *really* frustrating."

Educator Dr. Karen Beattie has turned down boards "that sought nothing more than a rubber stamp of approval of staff actions."

Community volunteer Karen Nessler shares that she won't get involved "if I don't feel like I could do a proper job or could have quality input."

Jim Zeiler, who has served on several volunteer boards, is clear about his involvement. "The board needs to have a defined purpose and meaningful work to complete. I'm not interested in just filling a seat."

WHEN ASKED TO SERVE ON A NONPROFIT BOARD, WHAT MOTIVATES YOU TO SAY YES?

Board prospects look at a broad spectrum of circumstances before accepting an invitation. Knowing what prompts them to say yes enables organizations to have conditions in place that prospects are looking for.

Marriage and family counselor Dr. Rosaria Upchurch considers the significance of the organization carefully before saying yes. "The board has to have a mission that is meaningful to me. I feel that I have to be able to have some impact. With other obligations, I have limited time, and the position must have major worth to me."

County government leader Dona Butler has several boxes she expects a nonprofit to check. "I have to find the mission of the organization to be appealing. If they are making an impact or have the ability to do so, then I find it compelling to serve. The reputation of the organization, the quality of board members, and the quality of staff are also factors in my decision."

University staff member Judy Rees gives thought to "who the other board members are and also how active they are."

Similarly, Jim McCauley, president of the International Association of Holiday Inns, says, "I would have to want to be associated with the current board members."

Attorney Rob Merrell goes further. He is more likely to say yes when "I have relationships with the other board members."

Land use planner Joel Ivey's qualifiers include "my belief I can contribute, my observation of the positive contributions of the board, and the opportunity to learn."

Utility company community representative Bob Coleman lists "what service the agency provides, the quality of the paid executive, and who else is on the board."

Board member Lynn McCoy considers "the cause of the organization first, then the time requirements, and what expertise I may add."

As with many respondents, whatever the cause, school district facilities director Pat Drago wants to be assured "that my participation will actually count."

If reasonable expectations such as these aren't met, a yes reply becomes a no, and a high-performing board prospect is lost.

HOW CAN BOARD MEMBERS BE USED MORE EFFECTIVELY?

Board members want—and expect—efficient and productive use of their time. Using board members wisely produces great benefit for your organization today and attracts even higher caliber board members tomorrow—creating ongoing benefit for your organization. The responses in this area fall into four categories: clarity on roles and responsibilities, use of their strengths, respect for their commitment, and simple appreciation.

Clarify roles and responsibilities

An interesting irony lies in the large number of organization executives who believe board members lack understanding of their roles and responsibilities. Board members are being held responsible for what they don't know and for experience they don't have.

Whose fault is that? Who recruited people without giving them the basic knowledge of what they're supposed to do? Who is responsible for making sure board members get the training they need?

Our survey participants agree that a better job must be done in establishing clarity for roles and responsibilities. As was noted earlier, getting actual acceptance of those duties is essential before prospects become board members.

Kentucky board member Norm Sanders advises, "Make sure each board member knows their responsibilities as related to goals of the organization."

Dona Butler believes that "underperforming boards are due to lack of training and a clear level of expectation being provided before service begins."

Joyce Hayhow recommends clear communication that includes a plan of action. "Sit down with each board member and lay out a chart of work for the year. Be it committee work or fundraising goals, it would be helpful for expectations to be communicated and agreed upon."

University trustee Matt Rearden counsels, "Give board members specific tasks, and then give encouragement that what is being done is helping."

Kevin Bowler similarly asserts that "roles must be clearly defined. Acceptance on boards must carry rules that, if not followed up on, result in loss of appointment."

The combination of task and reinforcement is echoed by John Flieder, who has an impressive history of board involvement. "Don't undersell what's expected of them, and have an understanding of what is feasible for the board members to accomplish. Recognition is needed for those who do their tasks well."

STOP THE NONPROFIT BOARD BLAME GAME

Play to their strengths

A farmer wouldn't expect a cow to do the job of a horse or vice versa. Recognize and take advantage of each board member's unique strong suits.

Chamber of commerce CEO Debbie Connors suggests, "Use the strengths of your board members, and don't waste their time."

Human resources executive Rob Brinkerhoff advises spending "more time getting to know the strengths of your board members and candidates for the board and capitalize on those strengths."

"Play to their strengths, have meaningful work for them to accomplish, and acquire different needed skill sets" on your board, recommends Jay Adams.

National youth basketball director Conrad Foss is of a similar mind. "Understand the board members' strengths, and then put them in positions to utilize their strengths."

Longtime Daytona Beach mayor Larry Kelly counsels, "Remember, board members are volunteers. Give each a task they can best perform."

With the experience of holding several elected offices, Fred Costello's belief expands on that thought. "Give definite options for service, as all board members aren't in the same situation."

Respect their commitment

When asked about how to create engagement and commitment in board members, the survey respondents offered many valuable suggestions.

To let board members know that they are held in high regard, convention and visitor's bureau CEO Lori Campbell Baker makes several recommendations. "Respect board members' time. Start meetings on time and keep them short and succinct. Use consent agendas when appropriate to have more time for items that require long discussions. Get board packets out early, not just one to two days prior to the meeting."

Be precise about board activities, says marketing and sales rep Laura Zublionis. "I find that, when you ask someone to do a specific task, that works way better than just saying assistance is needed."

Chamber of commerce lobbyist Jim Cameron focuses on involving board members in efforts that they know will make a difference. "Get them to do meaningful work. Not fluffy, feel-good stuff."

John Koberg's thinking is along the same lines. "Charge them with creating a solution to a particular problem and then have them be an integral part of the implementation."

Likewise, real estate agent Jim Tobin suggests "allowing the board members to be a part of the organization rather than just window dressing."

Auto dealership owner Bobby Thigpen believes in allowing board members to "contribute at their levels—meaning time, money, et cetera."

To create engagement, Penske Corporation executive Walt Czarnecki proposes offering board members these two possible roles: "Actively use board members as ambassadors in the community and also as advisers within the organization if they possess professional skill sets that could support a specific operational area."

Land use engineer Charlie Faulkner applies to board member relationships advice that is both sensible in the boardroom and excellent in life. "Put more effort into it. You get out of a relationship what you give it."

Show appreciation

Appreciation is currency that motivates volunteers. It's critical to remember that board members *are* volunteers! Make showing gratitude a priority. Although different people prefer to be recognized in different ways, everyone likes to feel appreciated.

CPA Dan Bolerjack wants leaders to remember how much the organization relies on maintaining board members' good will. "Organization leaders have to remember that these are volunteers. Board members don't work for the organization."

Financial advisor Jeffrey Brok believes in letting board members know that they are valued. "Show appreciation for the time and effort that they put in."

Foundation executive director Deb Gronvold suggests, "Have retreats or social meetings to make it feel more like something fun to do as opposed to a job."

Vince Carter Foundation executive director Ann Smith advises the straightforward route. "Listen to their advice and suggestions. Thank board members frequently and sincerely."

These candid critiques and suggestions reflect the experiences of board members who have been willing to share their feedback because they want to play a part in overcoming the frustration often associated with volunteer boards. Their views may not always align, but they give insights into perspectives likely held by your own board members and prospects.

Some in the nonprofit sector may consider these responses to be not particularly helpful, because they are fundamental and don't reveal anything new. I agree: They are basic. That is the point. If organizations were practicing the basics, the level of frustration with nonprofit boards would not be so high.

....

Develop your action steps

- What board member listening activity should you initiate?

- How will you address concerns expressed by board members?

- How will you follow up on board member suggestions?

PART 2

Get the Right People

4

RECRUIT BOARD
MEMBERS WITH PURPOSE
AND PROCESS

The Boys and Girls Clubs of Volusia/Flagler Counties in Florida (BGCV/FC) is among the best examples of an organization that totally nails board recruiting. This nonprofit has a clear expectation of engagement by their board members, and their record of recruiting success is amazing. Board recruitment at BGCV/FC is focused on individuals who can provide financial support through personal giving and through fundraising. They also seek influencers who have the ability to garner governmental funding.

Pinpointing their needs enables the organization to identify board prospects who meet their criteria and have demonstrated that they can deliver the desired results. The Boys and Girls Clubs of Volusia/Flagler Counties has been able to withstand the challenge of increasing demand for services in difficult economic times because of the solid performance of their carefully selected board members. The lesson here is that the key strategy for getting the right people on a board is recruiting with purpose and process.

Nonprofits have long been challenged by unmet expectations in board member engagement and performance.

Respected sources like BoardSource, GuideStar, and the Stanford Graduate School of Business Center for Social Innovation continue to report that a high percentage of nonprofits experience difficulty with successful board recruitment. These and other nonprofit research centers also identify other board needs, such as increased diversity, more strategic thinking, and a higher level of engagement in advocacy. Whatever the challenges, they can be most effectively and proactively addressed by starting with honestly evaluating current board recruitment practices.

If its board isn't performing as desired, an organization should face facts: The organization is probably recruiting the wrong individuals. If you want to condemn an organization to failure, it's easy: put the wrong people on the board. It is, in fact, a fundamental reason that board members themselves have identified for boards failing to meet performance expectations. They add that dedicated top performers are often turned off by a lack of performance by other members.

Moreover, poor board selection can be a three-strikes foul-up. First, the organization has self-sabotaged by having either an unproductive or, worse yet, a counterproductive board member. Second, the organization is preventing a board seat from being occupied by a positive performer. Third, and possibly worst, frustrated productive contributors are likely to head for the door. And the organization is then headed into a downward spiral.

These are why you should prioritize the board member recruitment process. The other questions are *When? What? Who? How?* and *When?* again. When should you start the process? What are your board needs? Who can meet them? How will you do it? And when else do you engage in this process? (I bet you already know the answer to that one!)

So why (yes, another why) don't boards get the individuals they need? The fault is with the recruiting process and not with the people being selected. To use a medical metaphor, you could say that frustration felt by board members and the organizations they serve is a symptom. Mishandling recruitment is the primary cause. Corrective action must be taken to find the cure.

Organizations must face the fact that they are contributing to their own board performance ills by not employing the proper recruiting process. That means there is no reasonable hope for relieving board performance-related frustration. Instead, make recruitment the proper priority: acknowledging its significance allows organizations to stop making what amounts to self-inflicted—and possibly fatal—wounds.

> **When board members aren't performing as expected, don't blame the people; blame your recruiting process.**

For you to attain consistently successful outcomes when filling board positions, recruitment must be a deliberate, structured, ongoing process.

THINK STRATEGIC RECRUITMENT—STARTING NOW

You should start this process right now. Working ahead to fill board positions cannot be emphasized enough. Waiting for the need to arise compounds recruiting mistakes that lead to almost certain engagement disappointment.

> **Use strategy, standards, and structure to identify best prospects.**

If your organization doesn't have scheduled action dates for filling future board vacancies, it should. Organizations should always be on the lookout for possible board members, have a pool of potential prospects, and have time allowed for proper vetting before final selection. Even when unexpected openings occur, if recruiting is an ongoing process, qualified candidates will already be identified.

Those who are invited to join a board because the time wasn't taken to find a truly qualified candidate are almost always sure to wind up being unengaged. Doesn't it make sense to avoid a board selection mistake of inviting someone who isn't able to fulfill expected engagement obligations by proactively working in advance?

The fortunate circumstance of having the right people sitting on your board doesn't just happen. It is the reward for creating a plan well ahead of time and working it consistently. When putting together your recruitment process, think strategically.

Having a deliberate plan allows you both to avoid organizational behaviors that lead to recruiting mistakes and to set yourself up to acquire the people best suited to your culture and your cause. Creating an ongoing structured recruiting process increases the likelihood that board members will not only meet but maybe even exceed your organization's performance goals.

The steps laid out here may sound a bit daunting, but they lead from one to the next in a logical way. Take the elements of this process and fill them out with the factors that are critical to your own organization. Then continue to evaluate your process. If a phase of the plan doesn't work well, be willing to recognize that and alter it.

MAKE FILLING BOARD VACANCIES A PART
OF THE STRATEGIC PLAN

Maybe the most obvious feature of a plan is that it takes time. Don't wait until the last minute to find warm bodies to fill board seats. This diminishes the importance of the positions and the people who fill them. An organization knows both when a board term is going to be up and that people sometimes leave unexpectedly; these are not surprises. There will be vacancies. When organizations wait until the last minute and then frantically search for board replacements, my experience has shown that they are willing to accept less than ideal prospect choices. Furthermore, they do not fully communicate expectations for fear the prospect will turn down the invitation. The predictable result is a board made up of slot fillers. Slot fillers may be nice people, but they aren't going to deliver on an organization's performance needs.

When it's time to fill a board vacancy, do these reactions sound familiar? "Okay, who are we going to get to fill this position?" "Who knows somebody?" "Who can we get?" Leaders should not be running around trying to catch the first warm body who can be talked into accepting their plea. Create a list—even a short one—of people you would like to consider for your board. Invite them to functions. Get to know them. Execute your deliberate plan. Be prepared when the next seat needs filling.

> Slot fillers may be nice people, but they aren't going to deliver on an organization's performance needs.

IDENTIFY THE WHAT, THEN THE WHO

The first step in a successful recruiting process is establishing what your board needs in the way of experience, skills, expertise, and ability to work in a team structure. An example could be that you need expertise in governance, which is becoming much more significant. Your board may need someone with legal and accounting backgrounds. Furthermore, executing good governance practices requires someone who is actively engaged and aware of both organizational performance and regulatory compliance.

As the world of nonprofits evolves, another example of desired expertise is in mergers and negotiation. If you are considering a corporate merger, you may want a board member who is experienced in acquisitions either from the corporate world or from another nonprofit. Perhaps you need to shore up membership, and you will look for someone who has experience in growing membership organizations with sales, marketing, finances, and accounting. Maybe you're going to launch a massive, new website presence, so you could really use some expertise for guidance in that area of technology.

When considering specific needs for your board, it's important to match recruitment with the desired objectives of the board and the organization. First determine what your board's needs are. Only then will you be able to seek out people who can meet them.

Let's look at three examples of the what driving the who.

Preachers don't do weather

I had a great friend in the world of racing—the late Reverend Hal Marchman—who, for decades, did all the invocations at Daytona International Speedway. One of the country's great sporting events is the day featuring two qualifying races leading up to the Daytona 500. They make for an action-packed, pressure-filled Thursday for race teams before the big 500-mile race on Sunday.

I remember vividly one particular race morning before our 11:00 a.m. start. The sky was pitch-black. Everyone was fearful a torrential downpour was imminent. Reverend Marchman and I were standing on the prerace stage when a worried fan rushed up.

"Reverend! You've got to do something about this weather!"

Always a quick thinker, the reverend replied, "Sir, I'm in sales. I'm not in management."

Reverend Marchman understood his expertise, his role, and his limitations. Likewise, make sure the people you choose for your board have the ability to do what you're asking them to do and that they understand their roles and limitations.

Learn from college sports recruiting

Recruiting by top college athletic teams provides an excellent model for developing a winning board recruiting process.

Successful teams are meticulously purposeful in their methodology. They devote time and resources to evaluating and cultivating prospects. Their approach identifies first their specific needs and then the prospects who meet them. They place a premium on selecting players who will be a good fit.

An organized system recognizes players with potential as early as youth league and tracks them through their senior year in high school. Coaches are assigned to monitor progress and develop relationships. Before offering a scholarship, the team must have a high level of confidence that a prospect will meet anticipated expectations.

Does the focus to keep an ongoing pipeline of quality players ready to fill a team's personnel requirements compare to nonprofit board selection? Absolutely. Unfortunately, the nonprofit board member recruitment process is often just the opposite of the intensive effort that goes into the quest for the best possible athlete. It shouldn't be.

Recruiting board members with a process similar to that of top-ranked teams has two definite benefits. First, organizations are more likely to fill board seats with individuals who will meet performance expectations. Second, the frustration caused by selection mistakes is diminished.

Renowned University of Kentucky basketball coach John Calipari explains results-focused recruiting in his book *Players First*. He has established a phenomenal record of success. The reason is his ability not only to consistently recruit top ranked prospects but also to get this collection of all-star players who are used to being the top attention getters in high school to share their spotlight with others and to buy in to his system.

Calipari says he is recruiting for a nontraditional program and needs special players who can meet its pressure-filled expectations. In every recruiting class, he's looking for championship players. And he knows what he wants from them: the prerequisite skills, physical attributes, work ethic, and mental and emotional maturity to play in the high-exposure world of Kentucky basketball, as well as a willingness to be coached and fit into a system that demands teamwork. With that template established, Calipari's recruiting effort then focuses on finding players who will be the best fits for the team. It's a very deliberate process built on identification of first the what and then the who.

What about your future-year board vacancies? Obviously, you will target some prospects who aren't now involved with your organization for possible recruitment. In addition, you can identify current members and volunteers who might be good candidates for your pool of potential future leaders.

Recruit Board Members with Purpose and Process

With your list of needs in mind, develop a prospect list that matches them. Look for team players who have attitudes that are about top performance and winning. With an eye to the future, execute a tracking system that identifies prospects that both meet your needs and exhibit your attitudes and values. Do as sports teams do, and initiate an evaluation process and relationship development to determine whether a future invitation should be extended. Sometimes, it should not be.

Not every sports team has the desire to compete for championships. What are the goals and desired performance levels for your board team? Do you want a team that's just an ordinary team with just enough members to put on uniforms and get on the bus? Or do you want a championship team?

Pay attention to naturally occurring qualities

Another example of a framework for the what comes from the world of man's best friends, dogs. My wife, Debbie, and I always enjoy watching the annual Westminster Dog Show. I am particularly intrigued by facts about each breed's natural inclinations and capabilities. The history of how dogs have been employed to accomplish a wide variety of tasks is fascinating. The unique personalities and skills of the breeds make each one ideally suited for taking on some pretty demanding challenges. Each one has the right tools for getting specific jobs done. For example, there are workers, leaders, protectors, and companions.

Westminster Dog Show announcers always stress the importance of considering a dog's distinctive competencies and personality as important factors when deciding which one to bring into a home. Some breeds are high maintenance and need to be handled with

55

kid gloves, while others are even tempered and do their job with a minimum of oversight.

The consideration process for matching qualities and abilities to a job can be applied to finding compatible members for your nonprofit or association board. What specific skills and talents does your board need? What personality traits will ensure that someone will be a good fit for the job? Are your prospective board members' demonstrated behavior and performance tendencies well suited to your organization? Will patience and extra training be required?

Likewise, it's also important to know what not to recruit for. For example, people are sometimes recruited simply because of their donation history or because they represent a funding source. Does what amounts to putting board seats up for sale ensure good governance or guarantee the organization will get the leadership it needs? It could backfire. The same is true for mere "names on the letterhead" who are nonperformers.

Identify your whats, and make sure your prospects suit them. You want each and every one of your board members to be your organization's best friend.

RECOGNIZE TRENDS INFLUENCING
RECRUITING SUCCESS

The world of nonprofits is changing dramatically, and the changes influence board recruiting. How will they affect your board?

The country is experiencing cultural and generational shifts. Pressures are increasing to meet service demands amid economic challenges, and governmental regulatory actions continue to grow. New and diverse circumstances are impacting nonprofits. In turn, these challenges are creating potential prospects with new demographics, causing organizations to revise board priorities and causing prospects to more carefully consider whether to accept board invitations.

Successful board recruiting requires organizations to constantly reevaluate their recruitment approach to ensure relevance in a continuously changing environment. If you stay aware of the trends, you can stay ahead of the challenges.

RESEARCH YOUR PROSPECTS' SUITABILITY

Once you have determined your whats—that is, your needs—it's time to focus on the whos—that is, the people best suited to meet them. Be prepared to put in the necessary time in prerecruitment screening. Do your homework. Unlike magical unicorns, performance-committed board member prospects do exist, but it takes planning and effort to find them. Working in advance of when vacancies occur allows for time to identify the most desirable prospects.

In their book *Prospect Research for Fundraisers*, donor research experts Jen Filla and Helen E. Brown gave me a lot of food for thought. They made me think about the similarity between finding donors and finding board members. To further explore this concept, I reached out to Jen. As she observed, "When there is an important decision to be made, it is worth investing time and resources to do proper research."

Indeed, dedicating time and resources to checking out the backgrounds of prospective board members provides a filtering structure that identifies and evaluates individuals most likely to be ready, willing, and able to meet board performance expectations.

"The objective is to obtain hard information," Jen says. "Due diligence is critical, because it allows decision makers to see facts about behavior, past performance history with other organizations, and whether or not an individual is aligned with your mission."

Organize your background work by first developing prospect criteria. Based on board performance expectations, what personality traits, skill sets, past board experience, history of giving, and other priority qualification categories are important for your organization's board candidates? Jen recommends the step of creating a score sheet with a grading column for each evaluation standard. To further facilitate the process, create and organize profiles of prospects for easy reference later.

WORK FROM REFERRALS; START WITH
BOARD MEMBERS

A smart place to start a search for board prospects is to consult with valued current and past board members. They know the demands and who among their friends are up to the job. They will refer those who they know will be a good fit and will perform as expected. In addition, people who are serving on a board are likely to recommend someone they would like to serve with and who has a shared passion for the cause. Moreover, this is likely to increase the enthusiasm of both parties for your organization.

Two other groups of people to ask for board recommendations are your staff and your past and present volunteers. They will know others who share interest in your cause. Furthermore, both volunteers and former staff members may be suitable board prospects themselves.

Other possibilities suggested by Jen Filla include your donor database, civic clubs, and chambers of commerce.

CONDUCT ONLINE RESEARCH

Background on most prospects is readily available with a little work. Internet search tools provide a wide range of information relevant to your board criteria and individuals on your prospect list. Social media platforms such as LinkedIn offer insightful individual profiles.

EVALUATE PROSPECTS THROUGH
PERSONAL INTERACTION

The significance of personal interaction cannot be overstated, because the most important evaluation comes from face-to-face conversation. Invite prospects to lunch and organization functions and to meet current board members. Spend time with them one-on-one. Dialogue should be structured so that the prospect's feelings about the organization and possible board service become readily apparent.

It is equally important for prospects to be engaged with asking their own questions to establish their comfort level for saying yes to a board invitation. Ask what questions they have about the commitment and your organization. Your prospects are evaluating the board position just as much as you are evaluating them.

Do not soft sell expectations. While this tactic may help reel in good prospects, it could also cause them to lose their initial enthusiasm or even to leave if they feel they are the victim of bait and switch. Confirm that they do indeed understand the expectations.

Don't listen for what you want to hear; listen to what they are saying. Are they committed to doing whatever the ask is? You must get to a point of commitment.

Jen urges those responsible for conducting research not to

overlook reaching out to the acquaintances of your prospects. She says peer reviews can be invaluable and may even include surprises that come from the people they suggest themselves. When speaking with prospective board members, ask for these references. Have they done with other organizations what you anticipate they're going to do with yours? Talking with these associates can validate your faith in your selections.

Once information has been collected, it's time to evaluate each individual. Now is when you fill in the score sheet that Jen recommends.

REMEMBER: BOARD MEMBERS ARE VOLUNTEERS

Although we will look at the volunteer aspect of being a board member later on, I want to touch on the fact here. The same basics for connecting with other volunteers apply to successful board prospect recruiting.

Anyone who works with volunteers knows that people don't necessarily join organizations because it's a good cause or because of a mission statement. They get involved for their own reasons. When considering prospects, take time to identify what stimulates their individual interests for serving as a board member for your organization. What are they looking for? What are their emotional needs? What personal connections do they have with the organization? What are their personal goals, apart from the organization's goals?

> People get involved in organizations for their own reasons. If you know each prospect's personal purpose, you can help them meet it.

Their motivations can range from a very personal connection to a particular cause to a need for the self-fulfillment of helping others to a connection to another volunteer or another board member. Evaluating these considerations will help determine potential for a good fit. If you know each prospect's personal purpose, you can help them meet it.

AVOID COMMITMENT CONFLICTS

How many boards can a person serve on effectively? An organization looks at prospects and says, "Okay, here's this high-profile individual in our community who's on five other boards. They are obviously pretty good. Why don't we invite them to add our board to their list?" Why indeed. Perhaps there are five reasons not to add them.

Probably, in any community, if you developed a matrix and listed all the board members for each local nonprofit, you would see a lot of names that are repeated. You would also see that many board members are sharing their community service time. But don't organizations really want a number-one priority relationship with their board members?

To reinforce this thought, I conducted a BoardSource discussion group survey that asked, "How many boards do you feel someone can be a part of and still be effective?" The overwhelming answer was "one." "Two to three"—if they were related to serving on a state or national board connected to their local board service.

How many number-one commitments for fundraising and governance and the effort it takes to serve on a nonprofit board can someone realistically and effectively make? When fundraising is an expectation, remember that there are limits to how much one individual can raise and how often that individual can hit up the same group of friends for contributions.

Why go after someone who is essentially working for the very organizations you're competing with for donor dollars? Rethink the premise that to get something done, you need to find the busiest person in town. When recruiting the busy person, are you willing to be a second, third, or lower choice for someone's time, talent, and treasure?

Here is another consideration: As you get to know your prospects, find out what their current commitments are. If they have many time-weighted responsibilities—whether personal or professional—you might want to wait for a more suitable time for them. If, however, their commitments, including serving on boards, are not so demanding, they may be viable prospects.

How many number-one commitments can someone realistically and effectively make?

AVOID SELECTION MISTAKES—NO FIXER-UPPERS

A good part of my career with NASCAR was spent under the direct guidance of NASCAR chairman Bill France Jr. One of the greatest pieces of advice he gave me was, "Hardy, anticipate and solve your problems in advance."

This valuable lesson can be applied to board member recruitment. If you are in a rush to fill a board position, it can be tempting to accept someone who comes up short on what the organization truly needs. However, if you have prospects who aren't going to perform the way you want them to, don't recruit them.

A willingness to overlook flaws in experience standards, performance ability, and other desired skills may be rationalized away by declaring the individual under consideration can be trained up or fixed later. This doesn't work. In fact, it can lead to a board's deterioration and downfall. How often does a relationship succeed when it begins with one of the parties overlooking the other's flaws or thinking the flaws can be fixed later? Is it rational to believe a recruit-them-now-and-fix-them-later approach will work for board members? If prospects need fixing, let somebody else fix them. Attract and invite those who fit nicely into your board position just as they are—not as fixer-uppers.

RANK YOUR PROSPECTS

After you have compiled all your information, take the time to rank your preferences. Grading your prospects will allow you to determine recruitment priority and whom to move off your list.

You may have more than one list using different parameters. For example, one list may be a general one to meet chronic needs. Another may address specific acute needs that exist now or will exist in the future.

Expect the unexpected. When a vacancy occurs, be prepared with the name of the next terrific addition to your board.

IMPROVE THE PROCESS

How can you improve your board recruitment process so that you get the right people? As I alluded to earlier, work as hard on recruitment as you do on fundraising, and you will reap the rewards of having capable, focused, and passionate board members, and your organization will flourish.

Assess and reassess each part of your process. As an example, who is responsible for board recruitment? Is it the executive director or other members of the organization? My experience is that when the CEO goes out and finds new board members and introduces them to the rest of the group, those new board members are seen as "belonging" to the CEO. Although it is not the intent, cliques form. Obviously, this runs counter to developing positive chemistry between board members when cooperation and collaboration are necessary for reaching group-oriented results.

Get your board members involved in suggesting names and doing interviews. The new additions become "our" board members. Continue to identify questionable steps in your recruitment process, and tweak as needed.

NEVER STOP RECRUITING

As with any college team that's successful year after year in spite of losing its top performers, you must keep recruiting great players and make sure you have the right players in the right positions on your board if you are going to be a championship team. Match people to your organizational needs and get the right people.

Although you don't recruit new board members on a daily basis, the recruiting process is continuous. Implementing this due diligence takes time. As Jen Filla cautions, "It is a mistake to think that good research is easy or fast."

Do the work before replacements will be needed for expiring terms. Even better, if you make this process an ongoing one, you'll be prepared for the unexpected.

Commit to the time and structured focus necessary for producing the high-value board members your organization wants. Work in advance. Just as college teams don't wait until graduation day to start thinking about

The board member recruiting process should be continuous.

how they will replace a departing player, don't wait until a vacancy occurs to begin your search for a board replacement. Make it a continuous process.

Teams competing for championships want championship-level players. Is settling for get-what-you-get results going to deliver what your organization needs? Of course not. Your mission deserves championship-level board members. Increase board engagement and reduce board-related frustration by developing and using a structured process that recruits performance-minded, well-matched board members.

....

Develop your action steps

- How would you grade your board recruitment process?

- What skills and experience are missing from your board?

- How can your board recruitment process be improved?

5

KNOW WHAT PROMPTS BOARD PROSPECTS TO SAY YES

When you are recruiting board members, what gets your prospects to yes? Knowing the considerations can help you in three ways. First, they provide insight into your organization's public perception. Second, you can capitalize on this information to correct misperceptions and make the most of your strengths. Finally and perhaps most important, you can refine your ask to attract the best board members for your mission.

The survey responses identified seven major considerations that influence a prospect's decision before making a commitment to yes. Contrary to what many believe, the survey results show that just having a good cause is not a persuasive enough selling point for board recruitment.

First, the strongest factor that encourages a favorable response is that the prospects feel a meaningful connection with the cause or organization that is both personal and professional. They want to evaluate whether or not you are a great fit for them before obligating themselves.

Second, the respondents want to know they will have an ability to make an impact and not simply be a name on a letterhead.

Please note: Prospects who want to lend their "priceless" names to your board without committing to attendance may not be worth the ink on your stationery. They are taking up space that could be filled by high-functioning members. In addition, they are getting credit for service that they are not performing.

Third, as perhaps you expected, time availability is an important consideration. However, my experience with volunteer recruitment tells me the real answer regarding time is whether or not someone is willing to commit their time to your organization.

Just having a good cause is not a persuasive enough selling point for board recruitment.

Fourth, who's asking makes a difference. The survey respondents shared that a positive response is much more likely when the ask comes from someone the prospect has a personal connection with and respects. So, when you send out your representative, get someone who knows the prospect to do the asking.

Fifth, another significant concern that affects yes decisions is the organization's financial soundness. There are people ready, willing, and able to rescue a sinking ship, but they are rare.

Sixth—and this may give you pause for thought—is public opinion of the current board members. Your board's current makeup affects its future makeup.

Seventh and finally is the public perception of your organization's strategic plan. Here is something really interesting to me: When I'm doing a session on strategic planning and the benefits of planning, everyone can give me a list of why planning is so important. But when I ask, "How many organizations in the room have a strategic plan or a plan of action or have updated a plan you've done previously?" not many hands go up. And then I ask, "Well, why not?" Without fail, the answer is, "Well, we just don't have time to spend time on planning." This is where I get a little put out. That's just ridiculous. A lack of planning negatively influences board recruitment. Board members tell me that they don't want to waste their time with an organization that does not have clear focus.

When identifying potential additions to your board, give careful thought to the perspectives offered by those who have already said yes. Paying attention to their insights will improve your recruitment efforts and will also help you find prospects who are more likely to make a positive contribution to your board.

Don't just say okay when a name pops up in a board meeting and you've got to fill a slot. If the prospect likes animals more than kids, they might not be the best Boys and Girls Club board member; go to somebody else.

Do your homework to determine if a prospect's interests, opinions, and background are a good match before you extend an invitation. Check each of the seven points gleaned from those who have taken on the task of doing good. Their insights will help you identify prospects who are a good fit and will be more likely to respond with an enthusiastic yes.

....

Develop your action steps

- Do you know the specific reasons each of your board prospects says yes?

- Is there a response pattern you can use to your recruiting advantage?

- How will you follow up to make sure reasons for an individual's yes continue to exist?

6

KNOW WHAT PROMPTS BOARD PROSPECTS TO SAY NO

When you are recruiting board members, what concerns prompt your prospects to say no? Yes, understanding why prospects say yes helps ensure successful board recruiting. But understanding why they say no can be equally important to the overall success of achieving your nonprofit's mission.

The answers should sound familiar. First, they provide insight on your organization's public perception. Second, you can capitalize on this information to correct misperceptions and make the most of your strengths. Finally, and perhaps most important, you can refine your ask to attract the best board members for your mission.

That's right. The answers of board members participating in my "Why Don't Board Members Do What They're Supposed to Do?" survey revealed that no could actually have meaning that goes much deeper than "not enough time" or "not having a connection with the cause."

The survey responses indicate that a board turndown may be symptomatic of significant organizational issues. The respondents cited these five specific red flag concerns as negatively influencing board prospect decisions.

- The board isn't organized, and its goals aren't clear.

- The current leadership is a turnoff.

- The current staff or board members are a turnoff.

- There's a financial cost, or there's too much fundraising.

- It's a board in name only, and not much would be accomplished.

Here are some suggestions to help discover why board prospects turn down invitations to join your board.

- Consider the possibility that your nonprofit's efforts are being compromised by a less than positive reputation or a damaging perception that needs addressing.

- Create a dialogue in your recruitment process that allows honest feedback when a board prospect isn't responding positively.

- Conduct a self-evaluation to determine possible causes when negative responses seem to be a trend.

- Recognize that when prospects say they don't have time, their real message could be that they don't want to spend time with you. Perhaps it's just that they have a cause that is a higher priority for them.

Learning the truth about your reputation in your community can sometimes be painful, but it must be done if you are to survive. Be willing to accept a candid assessment as constructive criticism and a first step toward corrective action.

Take the time to honestly evaluate your recruitment process and the kind of results you are getting. Are you attracting good people? Again thinking like a sports team, are you getting your top list of prospects, or are they going somewhere else?

Understanding why prospects say no is very important to the overall success of achieving your nonprofit's mission.

When prospects say, "I don't have time," "I don't feel comfortable raising money," or "I don't really have a close connection to this cause," don't pressure them into saying yes. Believe them when they tell you up front they don't really feel comfortable or capable of doing what you're asking. If you force a yes from reluctant folks who really have no intention of doing what you want them to do, whose fault is that? An offshoot of this principle is not to force people into leadership roles when they indicate that they don't want the job. It is asking for a poor result.

If you can see recurring themes—why your board prospects say yes and why they say no—use the feedback to its fullest. And don't dismiss individual insights that could make a huge difference in future recruitment and long-term success.

....

Develop your action steps

- Do you know the specific reason when a board prospect says no?

- Are your no responses identifying situations that need correcting?

- What action will be taken to correct those situations?

7

HAVE THE MONEY TALK

To say there is frustration associated with the topic of board members and fundraising would certainly be an understatement. Anyone involved with the nonprofit sector knows this is a major issue. It is common knowledge that nonprofit organizations routinely worry that their board members might not meet expectations for fundraising performance. Less common knowledge, my survey revealed, is the rarely discussed topic that board members, too, feel frustration over expectations. They also share that the way the expectation is communicated contributes to the frustration and that too much emphasis is placed on fundraising.

If frustration related to fundraising is shared by both board members and the nonprofits they serve, why, then, is there such a disconnect over the very critical role of board members and fundraising? To be clear, the fundraising role we are addressing here is the expectation that board members will make direct requests for contributions and not more passive tasks like providing introductions or participating in an event.

If an organization wants to resolve frustration issues and

successfully engage the board in fundraising, it must adopt a new approach: Don't assume board members will raise money. Nonprofits are headed in the wrong direction if they assume "it's the board's job to fundraise." Debate on this issue can get quite heated, and there is a mindset in some organizations that, in exchange for the privilege of serving on a board, an individual gets to give and raise money. Perhaps this thinking is based on best practice governance models that identify ensuring adequate finances or maintaining financial stability is one of the roles and responsibilities of all board members. This may be a recommended best practice, but it should be practiced with care. There is a significant difference between "ensuring and maintaining" and being obligated for direct fundraising.

AND THE SURVEY SAYS . . .

According to board member feedback, there are two specific reasons your board members aren't fundraising.

The first reason, as mentioned earlier, is that you have the wrong people, a continuing theme in the survey responses: If you want fundraising board members, get fundraisers. Here's a reality check for organizations that depend on direct solicitation by board members to raise money: Not everyone is a fundraiser. Not everyone is comfortable asking others for money, and many detest the thought. Nonprofits counting on board members to bring in necessary funds should stop trying to force square peg nonfundraiser personalities into fundraiser round holes. It doesn't work.

If you want fundraisers, get fundraisers.

If your organization needs its board members to be fundraisers, then make successful fundraising experience, skill, and willingness to deliver priorities when identifying prospects. Placing a greater emphasis on making sure you are recruiting actual fundraisers will reduce frustration with performance and will significantly boost your fundraising results.

Consider the areas of a potential board member's specific strength and focus. A person who successfully sells annual gala tickets may not be the high-powered fundraiser you need for a multimillion-dollar capital improvement campaign.

When fundraising is the priority, it is important to understand that passion doesn't automatically translate into fundraising willingness or ability. For one thing, not every person who is passionate about a cause is a fundraiser. I see this often. Some just don't have the necessary skills, experience, or contacts to successfully ask others for money. For another, I have seen board members who have strong feelings for a particular program and feel focus on fundraising is misplaced. They believe greater attention should be given to activities that provide services.

The point here is to not assume who will do what but to get the right person for the job. In this case, the job is fundraising. To ensure that you are getting the right person, incorporate these two critical elements into your board recruitment process:

Do your homework. What is the history of your prospects with other organizations? Do they deliver on fundraising commitments? Are they presently involved with other fundraising efforts? Do they have room for your cause?

Have a candid conversation. I can't overstate the importance of effective communication with board prospects regarding fundraising expectations. Be up-front and clear about the organization's needs and intentions, and listen for any hesitation or questions that would indicate a reason that an individual is not the performer you are looking for. Of even greater importance is getting a confirmation that the expectation is accepted.

The second reason—after having the wrong people—your board members aren't fundraising is that once-good fundraising performers lose their enthusiasm. According to the survey, board members report that they are turned off by a lack of accountability for those board members they consider not meeting performance expectations.

Board members may also be offended by the expectation of personal financial support. While this may seem to be counterintuitive, the survey participants cited this as a problem. Individual giving is a very personal issue. Don't assume your board members will be willing (or even able) to contribute or to contribute at a required level. Resolve potential issues with give-or-get policies in advance.

Here's another important cautionary note. Good fundraisers may or may not be your best governance-related board members. Sitting through board meetings, dealing with organizational policy, and involvement with other routine board business may not be how some high-level fundraisers want to spend their time. Furthermore, with the growing emphasis on a board's governance responsibility, organizations might consider a pragmatic structure that allows fundraisers to fundraise and those better suited for governance roles to assume oversight roles.

Organizations with clearly stated fundraising and personal giving policies that are understood and agreed to by board prospects are much more likely to avoid the frustration drama that many others experience.

There are four categories of fundraising board members:

- Those who come in with skills, experience, and willingness
- Those who, with training and motivation, will fundraise
- Those who once did and now won't
- Those who don't and never will fundraise

Your recruitment screening process should identify the first three types and whether or not they will fit your board member fundraising (and other) needs. If it's money you're looking for, selecting board members who fall into the fourth category can be avoided by implementing the suggestions throughout this book.

Organizations that want to continue their longtime success of direct fundraising engagement by their board members can help maintain positive results by keeping in mind the insights offered by the survey participants.

....

Develop your action steps

- What is your give or get policy?
- Who determines what your financial expectation is?
- Do you have an enforceable accountability policy for this expectation?
- Are you recruiting fundraisers?
- Do you have the money talk in advance?

Create a Positive
Board Experience

8

RECOGNIZE THAT
RELATIONSHIPS
ARE THE KEY

Strong, meaningful relationships are at the heart of creating a positive and productive board experience. How board members feel about their experience has a major influence on their level of engagement. If the combination of relationships and board experience isn't good, a previously committed board member is likely to become frustrated and, in turn, to disengage.

Anyone in a successful relationship, whether personal or business, knows the ingredients: trust, respect, attention, appreciation, time, dependability, and—perhaps most important—communication. Board members, relating why they don't perform as expected, have shared with me situations where they feel one, some, or all of these elements are missing or downplayed.

Furthermore, board members identify communication issues as causing much of their frustration. Often, an organization's expectations for board members don't match the expectations of the board members themselves. Assumed expectations are a prime example of a failure to communicate.

Whether you are a staff person or a board leader, when you are feeling perplexed and asking yourself, "Why don't those board members do what they're supposed to do?" evaluate your part in the relationship you are supposed to be nurturing. As a leader, be open to honest self-assessment. Ask yourself these four questions and then take appropriate action.

- How do I rate my relationships with my board members?

- How can communication with board members be improved?

- What actions can be taken to improve the overall experience of my board members?

- What behavior changes will contribute to a more positive relationship?

In the view of many organizations, solutions for solving frustration with board member performance revolve around "fixing" the board members. However, in failing or failed relationships, both parties usually share responsibility, and successful relationships take both parties working together. That being said, in the nonprofit board scenario, the board chair and the CEO of the organization must work together to resolve relationship issues.

Board members say they become discouraged when the nonprofits they are trying to serve don't work to develop positive relationships with them. Using this insight, shift the focus from fixing the board member to fixing the relationship. And a good place for nonprofit leaders to start is by looking at themselves.

BE PROACTIVE

The proactive approach of focusing on the actual problem—relationships rather than on the board member—ultimately reduces frustration for both nonprofit leaders and board members. To give more clarity to the feelings of board members, let's revisit insights from five of the people quoted earlier who responded to this question: "As a board member, what is your biggest criticism related to organizations and relations with their boards?" Their responses offer suggestions that can help improve board member relationships. You can't have good relationships with people if your lack of proactive communication tells them that you just don't respect them.

Lori Tolland of Ormond Beach, Florida, says that her biggest criticism is a "lack of communication of expectations" about the time she volunteers. Actively and proactively respect board members' willingness to serve.

"I believe openness about differences is essential," says Rusty Jessup, mayor of Riverside, Alabama. "Don't pretend there is not a problem. Never ignore the 1,000-pound gorilla in the corner. Don't sugarcoat anything for PR purposes. Close your meeting if necessary, but talk about the gorilla." Actively and proactively respect their intellect.

Former Florida State University president, T. K. Wetherell, feels problems can develop with board relations because "nonprofits often expect more and more of board members who have lives and businesses to run." Dr. Wetherell suggests, "Ask only when you need their help and limit the asks to something that can make a difference." Actively and proactively respect their time.

Penske Corporation executive Walt Czarnecki is an advocate of management and boards "working more closely on all issues—not just financial," as a way to improve board relations. Actively and proactively respect their variety of contributions.

Nebraska Chamber of Commerce and Industry president Barry Kennedy believes that it only makes sense for board members to receive "continuous communications on the progress of the organization." Actively and proactively respect their roles as policy and decision makers.

In order for it to work, respect must be mutual. If you don't show it in the many ways you interact with your board members, on what basis would you expect them to have respect for you? Heed this valuable advice from five very engaged board members. Acting on these suggestions will certainly help your organization strengthen its board member relations. Silence on these and other areas loudly tells board members that they are just being used.

APPLY GOOD CUSTOMER SERVICE PRINCIPLES

Businesses with a reputation for their long history of repeat customers owe their success to a commitment to excellence in customer service. Building relationships is at the foundation of treating customers in a way that motivates them to remain loyal to the business—loyal to the point where they could be described as fans.

> **Developing and nurturing positive relationships is essential to avoiding frustration with nonprofit boards.**

Exceptionally good customer service practices make people feel special. There is a constant demonstration that customers are valued and appreciated. Furthermore, customers feel confident that any concern they may have will be immediately dealt with to their satisfaction.

The business sector knows that consistently producing high levels of customer happiness translates into extraordinary customer retention numbers, which of course have positive impact on their bottom line. Moreover, for-profit practices that produce consistently exceptional repeat business can also benefit nonprofits. The values essential for a successful customer relationship are the same as those imperative for board members. Look at it this way: For a nonprofit or an association, board members are a distinct type of customer.

To provide insight on how good customer service practices could help develop relationships with board members, I reached out to two speaker colleagues who are recognized customer service pros.

Ruby Newell-Legner works worldwide with professional sports teams, major hospitality venues, and international events such as the Olympics and the Super Bowl. Her techniques for developing 7 Star Service can reverse negative opinions board members may have about their board experience.

Ruby advocates revolutionizing the fan experience in order to enhance customer loyalty and retention. Can you see how incorporating this philosophy would translate into reversing the lack of engagement that causes frustration? Wouldn't it be transformational if you could return once enthusiastic board members to their place of positivity and excitement for serving your organization? Even better, what about using these techniques to avoid turning valued board members off in the first place?

Ruby's approach focuses on an organization's leaders taking ownership for setting an example of exceptional customer service. "Leaders demonstrating and reinforcing expected behavior set the stage for inspiring others to adopt interaction practices that create a compelling experience."

She adds, "Educating and training on the importance of executing exceptional service will produce a cultural change that converts customers to fans who will as a consequence remain loyal to your cause."

Applying this principle, Ruby's advice is a message for both organization and board leadership. Place a priority emphasis on the importance of service to board members. Treat them like customers you want to keep.

Adapted from Ruby's 7 Star Service recommendations, these five actions will help build a platform for improving board relationships.

1. Discover what motivates your individual board members.

2. Engage board members by focusing on their experiences.

3. Break down barriers between staff and board members.

4. Develop leaders with a service mindset.

5. Encourage loyalty by rewarding it.

Donna Cutting, author of *The Celebrity Experience* and *501 Ways to Roll Out the Red Carpet for Your Customers*, also has a wealth of customer service strategies that will help with relationship building. Let's look at Donna's suggestions. How would your board members react if they felt like they received red carpet treatment from your nonprofit? Would such outstanding attention to detail and relationship building translate to increased engagement?

Donna's advice provides an excellent path to stopping the frustration felt by board members. Her methods for implementing her Red Carpet Service program will also help correct relationship issues between nonprofits and their boards.

Here are five tips based on Donna's insights to give your board members the star treatment:

Make them feel like family

People are attracted to your organization because it's something they believe in, and they want to feel like they are connected to the cause. Your entire staff should be aware who your board members are, so when they show up or call, they are welcomed by name and as an important member of the family. Spend some time educating your team on who your board members are and brainstorm ways to make them feel important and special.

Give them a sneak peek

Invite your board members to special events and give them a behind-the-scenes look at the inner workings of your organization. Let them in on special announcements before everyone else knows and keep them informed. A mixture of live events, social media groups, mailings, and email can be used for this purpose.

Keep in touch

Along those same lines, don't make every message to your board a request for money. Instead, find other ways of staying in touch. Send birthday messages or regular thank you notes. Donna uses "Today Is Your Day" cards that are sent to let someone know they are being thought of.

Involve the board

Ask your board leaders to send personal thank you notes expressing gratitude for board contributions.

Send welcome gifts

In addition to the typed thank you notes you send when new board members come on board, send them something that connects them to your organization—for example, an inexpensive trinket, a mug, or a story that shows how their involvement is making a difference.

Whether you are using 7 Star Service or Red Carpet Treatment, when you make people feel special, they will be more likely to stay engaged. Ruby's and Donna's solid recommendations let your board members know that they are valued and that their opinions matter. They will feel appreciated.

COMMIT TO TAKING ACTION

Building and maintaining good relationships require consistent commitment to executing successful relationship keys. It takes work for a single relationship and will certainly require more effort for the multiple relationships involved with a board.

The importance of taking action to maintain good relationships is reinforced by Glenn Ritchey, president and CEO of Southeast Automotive Management. Glenn has built a reputation for exemplary customer service at each of his car dealerships. He also has a history of service on more than fifty nonprofit boards over the decades and understands the value of creating a good board member experience.

This wide-ranging background makes him a perfect source for advice on how to use customer service principles as a tool for developing good board member relationships. Here are some of Glenn's insights:

"It's easy to say you want to initiate a practice of relationship building. It can be fun to have kickoff activities to introduce a new concept like this; however, the real challenge is in the actual execution and that's where many good intentions fall short."

He also notes, "Fulfilling the promise of building good relationships with your board members takes more than just talking about it. Actually delivering it and demonstrating it through your actions is difficult because it is work and it takes time. Building relationships should be reinforced with regularly scheduled one-on-one meetings between the CEO and individual board members. An individual briefing on the organization's operations and allowing time for questions and discussion on items of concern help make the board member feel important and appreciated."

Glenn acknowledges the difficulty of allocating the amount of time he advocates to individual board member visits; however, he shares that, from his experience, the results are well worth the investment.

To ensure your relationship efforts are working, Glenn offers this additional piece of wisdom: "Remember the old saying, 'You can't manage what you can't measure.' Establish how you will be graded on delivery and execution."

Avoid the surprise of finding out that a relationship is in trouble. Don't assume that just because you aren't hearing complaints or dissatisfaction that it means all your board members are satisfied. They could be holding on to a concern they haven't been forthcoming about.

BE OBSERVANT

Watch for changes in behavior that indicate that something is amiss. In meetings, pay attention to attitudes, comments, and body language. Keep track of participation in non-board-meeting activities and follow up on a noticeable record of absences. Consistently reach out to check the temperature with individual conversations. Ask for suggestions about how their board experience can be improved.

The frustration associated with board member performance won't go away until issues causing the frustration are resolved. Frustrated board members not satisfied with their board experience aren't going to be engaged. So, focus on fixing their frustration, and you may just find your own frustration with disengaged board members evaporating.

Positive and productive relationships go a long way toward alleviating potential frustration that in turn leads to disengagement. They create connectivity, which is important because individuals work better with others they know and trust.

Many issues that foster frustration can be attributed to situations that contribute to undermining relationships. Consider those we have identified and the solutions for avoiding them. Relationship building requires a commitment to nurturing that must be constantly reinforced. Organizations that invest time and effort developing relationships with board members and facilitating relationships among board members themselves will reap the benefit of unlimited positive performance possibilities.

....

Develop your action steps

- How would you rate relationships between your board and your staff?

- How can those relationships be improved?

- How would you rate relationships among board members?

- How can those relationships be improved?

- How can you create a better experience for your board members?

9

DON'T FORGET: BOARD MEMBERS ARE VOLUNTEERS

Showing appreciation for good performance doesn't have to be complicated. For example, it could be as simple as a text message or a mention during a board meeting. Don't wait too long. Acknowledgment of the behavior you want to recognize will be more impactful if it is timely.

To further reinforce the behavior you want to call attention to, refer to the specific action by the positive performer. Another example could be to provide effective recognition at the end of a board meeting. Thank, by name, those who asked valuable questions about a particular item on the agenda.

Remember that volunteers are volunteers—whether they are engaged in a simple task like picking up trash on a beach cleanup day or in the more complex role of serving on the board of your nonprofit or association. The scope of work may be different, and the level of responsibility may be higher for board members, but the blueprint is the same.

Organizations that work successfully with their volunteers consciously implement a well-developed management plan. Moreover, the key structural elements of a solid volunteer program should be included in a plan for managing board members. The same skills and practices are vital to both.

Whether picking up trash on a beach cleanup day or serving on a nonprofit board, volunteers are volunteers.

The Corporation for National and Community Service's annual survey, Volunteering in America, consistently reports that millions of people volunteer their time to worthwhile charitable and community causes. However, the report also shows that, each year, equally large numbers of service-minded people are giving up on their volunteer activities.

This creates a revolving door of volunteers, triggering a never-ending cycle of recruit, install, train, lose, repeat. If you could increase your volunteer retention rate, how much time, money, and inconvenience would that save you? More specifically, if you could increase your board member retention rate, how much stress would that save you? When an organization is faced with board member retention issues, the challenge may be symptomatic of significant problems. Think like a volunteer. Understanding the volunteer perspective is critical to reducing attrition. Here are eight actions that will help you avoid retention difficulties with your board.

SHOW APPRECIATION FOR GOOD PERFORMANCE

Neglecting volunteer fundamentals has a direct impact on board member performance, especially when it comes to showing appreciation for involvement. Board members have shared with me that they often don't feel valued for their board service. In fact, many say a lack of appreciation is a contributing factor for other board members not performing as expected.

In any relationship, what actions demonstrate that individuals are appreciated? Listening to them? Not wasting their time? Showing signs of gratitude and respect? These are some of the practices we have discussed that contribute to the positive feelings that come from being valued.

In February, my annual Valentine's Day social media message asks, "Are your nonprofit board members feeling the love for their service?" Many indicate, "Not so much," which reinforces the importance of not overlooking board member recognition. Treat your board members like the high-value volunteers they are. After all, they are charged with responsibility for making the mission happen, and many are also financial supporters—so that "thank you" has a double benefit. Board members, like your other volunteers, are more likely to perform as desired when they know they aren't being taken for granted.

MAKE SURE YOUR RECOGNITION IS WORKING

A separate facet of recognizing effort is that it has to be done correctly to be effective. Of equal importance to the recognition is matching your appreciation to the recipient. Have you ever considered the possibility that your well-intended volunteer recognition of board members might not be as well received as you assume? I have spent some time studying personality characteristics, and it has given me a greater understanding of how various personalities can react quite differently to an affirmation designed to be nothing but positive.

Individuals' responses to recognition of their volunteer activity—or anything else—depend on their personality traits. Because different personalities naturally respond in different ways, your attempt to motivate could have the opposite effect. Before blindly handing out recognition or tokens of appreciation that could counterintuitively be a turnoff, first determine exactly what will inspire continued and enthusiastic involvement.

For example, if someone is a shy type, a public display of appreciation could be a source of embarrassment. On the other hand, for an outgoing personality, a lack of celebratory attention might be a huge disappointment. In both situations, the volunteer doesn't get the benefit of the all-important—and appropriate—recognition. And if volunteers don't feel appreciated—or if your efforts are off-putting—they often head for the door.

A simple email, a social media shout-out, a mention in a newsletter, or a thank you in a board meeting reinforces how much someone's efforts are appreciated. And of course, the personal touch of a handwritten note is always good, whatever the other larger or smaller gestures may be.

Whether a board member prefers an inexpensive plaque or that the cost be spent on the cause, it is critical to know who prefers what. I was once given a donation check to deliver to a local charity on behalf of one of our corporate executive officers. My instructions were very clear: "Hardy, if you come back with a plaque, you're fired! I want every dollar going to help someone!"

It is certainly important to respect someone's personal preference regarding recognition. Remember, however, that we're all human and have some form of ego that both values and requires that you are paying attention to those inclinations.

How do you determine people's appreciation preferences? Conversation and observation, both in and out of the boardroom, reveal important clues to what form of recognition is likely to be most effective and actually preferred. If you would like the benefit of more in-depth knowledge of an individual's preferences, consider the advantages of obtaining the insights that personality assessments can provide.

Communicating appropriate thank yous and acknowledging the value of someone's service should be routine. Instead of saving your display of appreciation for a big annual event, make it an ongoing activity. The better you make them feel, the longer they will stay engaged.

BEAR IN MIND THAT PEOPLE GET INVOLVED FOR THEIR OWN REASONS

Recognizing that individuals make involvement decisions for their own reasons is fundamental to understanding your volunteers. Interestingly, those reasons may or may not be about your good cause. Moreover, your good cause might not be enough to keep them if they are considering whether to stay or leave.

Take time to understand why your volunteers signed up. What is their true purpose for wanting to participate with your particular organization? They may have a need that relates more to a personal reason, and your organization or cause provides an opportunity to meet it. Are you fulfilling their need? If not, chances are good that these are volunteers you'll lose.

How well do you know your board members? What do you know about their families, their birthdays, their hobbies? Can you describe what they do for a living other than name their places of employment? The challenge for you is this: Know their personal reasons for being involved with your organization.

Saluting a great scoutmaster volunteer

I like to share the dedication of a volunteer who had a tremendous influence on me and what motivated him. One of my great experiences as a young boy growing up in Talladega, Alabama, was to have the opportunity to be a part of Boy Scout Troop 39, led by scoutmaster "Uncle Ralph" Bynum. As young teenagers, my fellow scouts and I were often more focused on what mischief we could get into—during our campouts on Cheaha Mountain in the Talladega National Forest and while hiking the Odum Scout Trail—than on paying attention to Uncle Ralph. Never to be deterred, he and his assistant, Tommy Huhn, diligently kept us on the right path.

Uncle Ralph had sons who had been scouts, but he didn't leave when they did. Instead, he devoted thirty-plus years of his vacation time to helping guide boys from other families. He was a wonderful, positive, and much needed influence in the lives of countless youngsters in that community for more than three decades. Beyond impressive.

Many years have passed since those youthful days in scouting. I can now recognize and am certainly grateful for the impact Uncle Ralph had on my life. I'm pretty sure that, at the time, not many of his scouts stopped to think about why he gave the dedicated service that he did.

Later, his wife Sibyl shared with me what motivated him. "He felt that all boys who wanted to be a part of what scouting had to offer should have that opportunity. It was his personal mission," she said. For Uncle Ralph, teaching scouting's life lessons was his life's passion.

Volunteering gave what Bear Bryant didn't

Another example of a volunteer with a personal reason for his dedication to helping others is that of my friend Ken James. Ken's motivation wasn't readily apparent, and it wasn't something he shared with others.

October is college football time, and one of the greatest games ever has to be the 1969 Alabama–Ole Miss game. On black-and-white screens across the country, a national television audience watched one of the first prime-time televised college games. The nation saw a fantastic quarterback duel between the Crimson Tide's Scott Hunter and Ole Miss great Archie Manning.

The Tide came away with a narrow victory, and one of their top performers was defensive end #83, Ken James. Ken's assignment was to pressure future Hall of Famer Manning, and he chased the elusive quarterback all game long on that hot, humid Birmingham night.

I got to know Ken through our involvement in the Alabama Jaycees (now known as JCI-USA). He agreed to serve on a team of program managers during my term as a state vice president. His role was to spend a year traveling the state promoting our programs, and he, along with the rest of our team, did an outstanding job. Ken took on volunteer work with the same relentless commitment he gave to making life miserable for opposing quarterbacks.

At the conclusion of our year-end awards ceremony, when Ken's outstanding performance was recognized, I watched as the big, tough, former Crimson Tide football player wrapped his huge arms around his petite wife Debra in an emotional embrace. Still very clear in my memory is seeing Debra come over to me, in tears herself.

"You just can't imagine what the Jaycee experience has meant to Ken," she said. "This has been the first time, including playing for Coach Bryant, he has felt appreciated. That is why he has worked so hard."

There is no doubt Ken worked hard as one of Bear Bryant's players. But his dedication as a volunteer produced an even higher performance level. Ken did not ask for acknowledgment and appreciation, and he taught me a valuable lesson about the impact of simple recognition. What I also learned was the importance of understanding that volunteers will sign up and stay involved because of personal connections.

Uncle Ralph and Ken James could be considered the gold standard; organizations struggle to find and retain volunteers like them. When you are fortunate enough to have board members like Uncle Ralph and Ken, work hard to keep them.

How you keep them is by identifying the individual needs that influence their involvement. Understanding what your

Volunteer 101: Know their why.

volunteer's personal connections are to your cause and making sure those needs are being met will help your organization benefit from dedicated commitment like that of Uncle Ralph and my friend Ken James.

CREATE CONNECTION PERSONALLY

People want to feel connected. Work to build personal relationships with your volunteers. Talk with them before and after meetings. Seek out their opinions in person or by phone. If you don't know them—and they don't know you—you'll lose them. In addition, foster ties between volunteers. These relationships develop and strengthen connection to your organization and will keep your volunteers involved; working with friends is a major motivator. When new people come on board, create opportunities that ensure that they are made to feel a welcomed part of the organization.

AVOID SINK-OR-SWIM MANAGEMENT TECHNIQUES

Sometimes organizations put board members in a leadership role without providing proper direction. This common occurrence is a big contributor to frustration and increases the chances of failure. People don't volunteer to be frustrated. They obviously don't sign up to see their efforts fail. This negative experience contributes to turnover.

You suffer two consequences. First, you lose valuable volunteers. Second, your organization also has allowed an important activity to be unsuccessful by failing to step in to ensure the success of those in leadership roles. Both are avoidable.

Whether those taking on leadership responsibilities have been there for a while or have just arrived, provide them with guidance, background information, training, or assistance from those previously serving in the same role. Don't let your hopes and plans for your volunteers sink; buoy them with the oversight necessary to accomplish your desired results.

DON'T DELEGATE AND FORGET

In a similar but different scenario, when board members take on direct responsibility for an event, a project, or specific board activity, organization leaders sometimes assume those being given the responsibility understand the task at hand and have the ability to get it done. Don't assume. Keep tabs on progress until the task is complete.

As with the sink-or-swim technique, delegating and forgetting is a recipe for disaster. Again, engaging in this behavior risks both loss of the volunteer and failure of the activity. Regardless of results, the volunteer's experience is almost certain to be frustrating. Unfortunately, there is a consistent pattern of volunteers who persevere, get the job done, and then quit because they feel abandoned.

When board members take on responsibilities, avoid potential negative results with these six tips for delegating successfully:

- Don't assume. Have ongoing conversations so you have a comfort level that your volunteer understands the task, is committed to it, and carries it out.

- Ask specific questions, such as *What's the completion date? Who signed up? What sponsors have committed? How many tickets have been sold?* and *How much has been raised?* Don't accept nonspecific answers like *It's going well.* and *Everything's fine.*

- Be a good listener and observer. Pay attention to signals that indicate your volunteer is struggling.

- Capitalize on each opportunity to recognize good effort. Positive reinforcement is a powerful motivator and goes a long way toward keeping volunteers engaged.

- Be ready to provide assistance when needed.

- Follow up and get real-time evaluation. Make needed adjustments so tasks remain on track for success right up to the desired conclusion.

If you delegate and proactively follow up with board members on their assignments, your missions will be accomplished. You will also help ensure that these volunteers have a positive experience, and you will avoid unnecessarily adding to volunteer board member retention issues.

AVOID BURNOUT

Loading up an eager performer who won't say no is a sure way to create burnout. It is easy to give tasks to a new volunteer who is willing to say yes. But how many times have you seen those shining stars flame out in a short period of time? Keep that performer around longer by consciously spreading the work around instead of always turning to the easy yes person.

Just like staff, volunteer board members are working to help those who have suffered misfortune, aiding victims in need of care, and finding solutions to someone else's problems. These dedicated volunteers deal with situations that can range from the simple to the complex and, often to the tragic.

The pressure and stress can be mentally, physically, and emotionally challenging. Even the most compassionate board member can feel the cumulative impact of such a demanding volunteer role. Unfortunately, the intensity of this already stressful environment is growing. While budgets are being cut and calls for help are escalating, nonprofits are being pushed to do more with less. So, who keeps your board members from burning out? The answer could be you.

As a high school basketball player, I was barely good enough to make the team, and my prospects for actually getting into a game were close to nonexistent. In spite of my bench-warming role, my three younger sisters showed up at games to loudly cheer for their brother. Their pleas to "Put Hardy in!" didn't persuade the coach but did totally embarrass me.

Through the years, my sisters have continued their encouragement. They recognize a need and offer support. My once youthful embarrassment has grown into appreciation and the realization of how fortunate I am to have such great cheerleaders in my life!

You, too, can have a positive influence on those you work with by being a cheerleader who provides volunteers with a much-needed boost. Help create a supportive environment that will assist in recharging those whose batteries are running low. Offer words of encouragement to those dealing with a particularly difficult situation.

Recognize when someone may be struggling in their volunteer role, and help find a way to temporarily lighten his or her load. An act of kindness will go a long way toward deflecting frustration, fatigue, and even burnout. Acknowledge those who are making a difference. The feeling of being appreciated is a powerful motivator. Champion the effort to get everyone working together as a team. Celebrate the individual and collective successes your organization is having so each person can share in the glow of accomplishment.

People who work to meet the needs of others are indeed special. But even those who help others need help and deserve recognition and encouragement themselves. My sisters were—and are—consistent cheerleaders who let me know I was not languishing alone. A sister can be a great cheerleader. And you can, too!

VALUE YOUR VOLUNTEERS

Volunteers who sign up for involvement with a nonprofit or an association board are anticipating a positive experience. When they don't find that gratification, they are frustrated, and, in turn, the organization they serve is frustrated by the lack of engagement that results when previous enthusiasm is lost.

Apply these action strategies in order to create a foundation for better relationships with your volunteer board members. You will create a positive board experience, enhance board performance, and increase board retention.

....

Develop your action steps

- What action can you take to identify your volunteers' why?

- How can you make sure each volunteer's why is being met?

- How can recognition of your volunteers be improved?

10

KNOW YOUR
BOARD MEMBERS

My work with nonprofit boards was—and continues to be—influenced by a personal experience, one that has made a lasting impression. New to the board of a local nonprofit, I took a seat at my first monthly meeting. A board member next to me leaned over and asked, "Hardy, do you know who the person sitting across from us is?" As the newest board member, I couldn't help but think it odd that veteran board members didn't know each other. Have you ever been in a similar situation?

According to BoardSource's *2017 Leading with Intent* and corroborated by the 2021 version, it's essential that nonprofit board leaders build a positive culture in order to reach consensus and compromise. The report states that this happens more easily when boards have the ability to work collaboratively.

Positive relationships are the cornerstone of successful and productive interaction among CEOs, board chairs, and board members. However, it's difficult to have productive and positive relationships when you don't know someone well. To get beyond casual acquaintance status to real connection, you must truly know them. Not doing so can create incorrect assumptions that contribute to misunderstandings and negativity in the boardroom.

Often, there are contributing factors that create barriers to personal connection. Geographical separations are typical among state, regional, and national organizations, often limiting in-person interactions. And at no time has this been more common than during the COVID-19 pandemic. While board meetings conducted via conference call may be a necessity, they're not necessarily conducive to relationship building. Using video conferencing is a better option for enhancing personal connection.

Don't stop there. Develop additional creative workarounds so that board members learn about each other's interests and backgrounds. Encouraging individual communication among staff, the board chair, and board members will also help to strengthen these relationships.

Creating opportunities for face-to-face contact is beneficial, when it is practical to do so. Based on my own experience—even among local organizations—introductions should be intentionally facilitated when in-person meetings are not the norm. For example, table name cards, individual name tags, and introductions at meetings are simple but effective techniques. Sharing a member's mission moments is an activity that provides valuable insights into individual motivations for serving on a particular board.

I've experienced board meetings when the single purpose appears to be to get in and out as quickly as possible. I bet you have, too. The business at hand is important, and so is encouraging pre- and post-meeting socializing that helps to develop all-important connections. Similarly, committee meetings and even board social events can create informal settings that are more favorable to relationship building.

Knowing others well creates a foundation of trust and facilitates working as a collaborative team—which has a cumulative positive influence for the board. Being intentional about knowing others allows you to communicate with them according to their communication preferences, which makes those communication efforts much more effective.

THINK LIKE THE COWS

A slap in the face from a wet and smelly cow's tail: that was my daily greeting from the first of more than 200 cows that needed to be milked. I worked on my family's dairy farm through high school and college, but the twice-a-day milking routine never came easily for me. Summers were stifling hot, and winter mornings at 3:00 a.m. were often below freezing.

The workers stood in a pit that placed the cows at chest level. It felt like daily combat, with the cows definitely having the advantage! My arms and hands were targets for quick kicks, and my face was the object of nonstop tail swats.

For some reason, the longtime veterans of the dairy didn't seem to have the difficulties I did in getting the cows' cooperation. One particularly frustrating morning, an experienced coworker offered some advice that, at the time, I laughed at. But, later, I realized it was actually quite profound.

"Hardy, you have to learn to think like the cows if you want their cooperation." This gave me valuable—and transferrable—insights into bovine thinking that helped me improve my ability to work with cows—and with people. Put yourself in their position.

Nonprofit leaders seeking to improve relationships with their board members can benefit from this dairy barn wisdom. Think like a member of your board. It can help foster relationships among members of the board and, moreover, can apply to many other types of associations and interactions. Bonus: This mindset also works with your other relationships and interactions.

ENABLE SUCCESS BY IMPROVING CONNECTION

We often make the mistake of assuming we know what others want. I thought that all the cows needed was to be fed and milked, but they obviously responded better to a more informed approach. As humans, we can get so focused on the work to be done that we don't take the time to better understand those we are working with. As a result, collaboration and achieving goals may suffer.

But can you think like others if you don't really know what's important to them? This reality applies to how well you know your board members, how well they know you, and how well they know one another. Part of better knowing others is understanding what's important to them. I found out that assuming can lead to mistakes.

Is your nonprofit one that assumes it knows the preferences of supportive board members? If so, how certain are you that your assumptions are correct?

MOMS AND HAIR DRYERS

When I was a youth basketball coach for a team that traveled to out-of-town tournaments, I depended on parental involvement. The parents took on numerous tasks, like preparing meals and washing uniforms. They also accepted my near-fanatical insistence on following a well-organized schedule. For the most part, they also tolerated my coaching.

I learned a valuable lesson when I booked rooms for one particular tournament. A hotel offered a room rate that was a few dollars less than what the families had paid previously. Although the accommodations were of lower quality than they had been accustomed to, I assumed the families would be happy with the less expensive rate.

At breakfast the first morning, I faced a group of upset mothers. The savings on room rate meant reduced amenities, including no hair dryers. The mothers were not happy! The group of people I needed support from was not in a cooperative mood. Until that day, hair dryers had not been on my list of concerns.

Applying this lesson, nonprofits should ask for input and opinions regarding significant issues from their board members before making event (and other) organizational decisions. Consider carefully; longtime supporters could either be turned off or be motivated to higher levels of support.

Many details can influence enthusiasm for an event—for example, schedules, formats, menus, pricing, entertainment, and location. Sometimes, a detail that seems insignificant to you could be a major one to board members whose participation is critical for a successful event (again, as I learned the hard way). This kind of forethought should be given to board meetings and any other activity that includes board participation or buy-in.

I learned to be smarter about implementing money-saving ideas that had not been thought out. My basketball moms wanted hair dryers, and they were willing to pay more for them.

With regard to each board-related activity and interpersonal communication, make no assumptions. Take the time to find out what is important—and not so important—to your supporters. Learning to think like others—and not assume you know their preferences—is a good place to start the process for getting to know someone better.

BE A GOOD LISTENER

Another important strategy is to keep in mind the significance of listening. It's the most important element to successful communication because it provides an opportunity to delve more deeply into understanding another person. A demonstrated commitment to listening can develop a foundation for fostering positive, long-term relationships.

Both staff professionals and volunteer leaders can significantly reduce board-related frustration by becoming good listeners. When you practice active-listening techniques, you can greatly improve interaction with others.

Speaker and extraordinary leadership development consultant Barry Banther is the author of *A Leader's Gift: How to Earn the Right to Be Followed*. As a leader, Barry believes in bringing out the best in others. Over time, he developed the skills that made him successful in leadership roles. Today, his distinguished consulting practice is built on sharing what he has learned, which he admits has not come without painful mistakes along the way. He credits his success to learning to listen.

A commitment to developing and practicing active-listening techniques greatly improves interaction with others.

There are many lessons in *A Leader's Gift*. Among the most important are why and how to listen, what to listen for, and how to apply what is learned. Establishing lasting relationships requires honest communication. Having solid rapport greatly influences how people respond to those in leadership roles. Furthermore, being committed to listening shows genuine interest and demonstrates that you are ready to put others first. It's the secret sauce in the recipe for making important communication work.

How does this play out? Giving people the sense that you are paying attention to what they are saying elevates their self-confidence and self-worth. Feeling appreciated and believing that their opinions matter, they may even become motivated to perform at levels they may have never previously reached. Finally, listening creates an opportunity for you to recognize when a word of appreciation can reinforce a desired behavior or when encouragement could elevate someone who is struggling.

According to Barry, followers are attracted by openness, investment of time, willingness to listen, encouragement, and appreciation on the part of staff. He has identified these five skills for becoming an effective listener.

- Focus on the individual. Put aside any other activities, and don't allow any distractions to giving your undivided attention.

- Avoid judgment. Don't predetermine or assume what someone is attempting to communicate.

- Go deep with questions. Questions provide more information and greater awareness.

- Search for misunderstanding. Recognize that misunderstanding is a natural occurrence; listen for it, and proactively work to clarify and correct it.

- Show appreciation for honest dialogue. Responding positively rewards the behavior you want to encourage.

Barry has crafted four questions designed to produce specific information during a conversation that will get someone to provide deeper insight on their thoughts.

- How do you mean that?

- Can you give me an example?

- Why is this important?

- How will this affect us?

Barry's questions have a two-way benefit. The person asking questions is getting information that will be useful for relationship building. The person answering the questions will realize that their opinions matter. This, in turn, creates a connection that can increase engagement commitment. If you aspire to be a great leader, give yourself a leadership gift by applying these lessons from Barry Banther on how to be an effective listener.

It's also important to remember not to treat a conversation as if it's a competition. Don't be ready to pounce at the first opening to interject your thoughts and comments.

What can you learn by being a devoted listener? A lot! Listen for how others feel, what their interests are, how they want to be involved, what's important to them, and what they need to succeed. You will discover their concerns, ideas, and thoughts, and even why someone isn't performing as expected. This information allows you to respond appropriately with corrective action, necessary coaching, or development of a performance improvement plan.

Can you see how people will be much more inclined to become engaged when they believe that what they're doing is important and that they are supported and respected? Listening is a powerful leadership tool: When people know you put them first, positive results will follow.

RECOGNIZE PERSONALITY CHARACTERISTICS

Has your organization had board members you consider difficult? When individuals don't know one another well, the stage is set not only for misperception but also for inaccurate labeling. For example, board members who often ask challenging questions may be tagged as difficult and disruptive. But are they really?

The book *Make Difficult People Disappear*, by speaker Monica Wofford, points out that there is quite a difference between the truly difficult and the merely different. It's possible that someone could be mislabeled as difficult just because they don't fit the same personality mold as other board members. Conversely, a truly difficult board member can be disruptive, bully others, or attempt to dominate an organization. This type of individual's negative behavior affects participation by other members and can cause harm to a group's good work.

Consider this: A board member who is different can add diverse thought. Diversity has the potential to offer new approaches, opinions, and experiences that can benefit your board's critical thinking. With a little bit of effort on your part, you can turn perceived negativity into a world of new ideas.

For board members who present a personality challenge, try these eight suggestions:

- Set up getting-to-know-you time to develop a better understanding of their perspective.

- Recognize that people process information in different ways. Examine your communication techniques to ensure you are communicating effectively.

- Consider that there may be issues outside the boardroom that are influencing attitude and disposition.

- Communicate that their opinions and feedback are appreciated and that they are adding value to board conversations. The opportunities that their contributions provide may be just what your organization needs to move forward.

- Improve facilitation skills for yourself and your board chair in order to improve the handling of meeting participation.

- Consider the possibility that someone may not be fully informed. Reexamine your new board member orientation and your procedures for introducing new ideas and projects to the board.

- Don't automatically assume you know others' reasoning for asking a certain question or taking a certain position. Encourage further explanation. Take time to fully understand their viewpoints.

- Demonstrate patience and allow yourself to be more tolerant of various personality characteristics before dismissing someone whose new perspectives could actually be a real asset.

Recognizing the difference between dealing with difficult and appreciating different can be a tremendous benefit for your organization. Follow these tips to help make the different board member a valuable asset to your board.

Knowing an individual better will reveal whether or not their inquiries are motivated by a desire to help. A board member who is willing to ask thought-provoking questions that others aren't willing to ask is helping the board stay in line with good governance responsibilities. The knowledge that their comments are coming from a place of sincerity will have a positive effect on how others around the board table react—and interact.

FACILITATE RESULTS BY MATCHING GOALS AND PERSONALITIES

Knowing individuals well enough to select them for your board will help you maximize their distinctive strengths and interests, rather than mistakenly assuming they will take on whatever duties are assigned.

For example, the daily routine of individuals in CEO roles may not find them engaged in hands-on execution of task-oriented activities. Why? Because they're in the practice of delegating. The big-picture-thinking CEO could be perfect for providing strategic guidance. If you want task-focused board members, consider individuals more aligned with that type of activity.

Understanding personality characteristics will provide clues about members' likely engagement response to your expectations. Pair current board members with assignment requests that are compatible with their individual characteristics and work styles.

Wouldn't knowing this type of information in advance help

prevent potential frustration with board members who've been given mismatched assignments? Successfully navigating these circumstances is a benefit of knowing the people you're dealing with.

To help develop a higher level of appreciation for recognizing different personality characteristics and their associated behavioral traits, I recommend taking a brief self-assessment. This particular self-evaluation is a product of the CORE Multidimensional Awareness Profile, in which I am certified. This is a great tool for a staff and board development activity.

Although the following is not a full assessment, and it doesn't have the benefit of evaluation and individual consultation by a certified consultant, it will provide insight into how your board members see themselves. Self-perception is important because it impacts how they show up in the world. After completing the exercise, you can match up your results with the accompanying attributes chart.

CORE SNAPSHOT

Read each horizontal set of words and make one selection from either column A, B, C, or D. Select the one that describes you most or most often. Once you have finished, record your total for each column. When added together, the totals should equal 18. If they do not, please check to be certain you have made a selection in each row.

A	B	C	D
___ Leader	___ Planner	___ Team Player	___ Motivator
___ Decisive	___ Meticulous	___ Flexible	___ Enthusiastic
___ Direct	___ Technical	___ Supportive	___ Outgoing
___ Problem Solver	___ Structured	___ Adaptable	___ Energetic
___ Driven	___ Precise	___ Sympathetic	___ Spontaneous
___ Goal Directed	___ Scheduled	___ Laid-back	___ Sociable
___ Independent	___ Sensible	___ Compliant	___ Imaginative
___ Ambitious	___ Organized	___ Follows Rules	___ Unpredictable
___ Need a Challenge	___ Need Order	___ Need Stability	___ Need Freedom
___ Bold	___ Careful	___ Easygoing	___ Persistent
___ Action	___ Logic	___ Reassurance	___ Excitement
___ Take Charge	___ Cautious	___ Patient	___ Approachable
___ Impatient	___ Perfectionistic	___ Indecisive	___ Forgetful
___ Competitive	___ Orderly	___ Cooperative	___ Convincing
___ Self-directed	___ Focused	___ Extra-Miler	___ People-oriented
___ Restless	___ Skeptical	___ Undirected	___ Undisciplined
___ Influential	___ Time Conscious	___ Good Mediator	___ Inspirational
___ To the point	___ Specific Details	___ Helpful	___ Interesting
Total _____	Total _____	Total _____	Total _____

CORE SNAPSHOT TOTALS

Column A_____   Column B_____   Column C_____   Column D_____

The CORE Snapshot was designed to provide a quick look at your current self-perception. It is single dimensional and may or may not be an accurate representation of your true nature. Early conditioning or current circumstances may have altered your self-perception. An altered self-perception can result in lowered energy levels, inefficiency, discomfort with self and others, lack of focus or direction in life, increased stress levels, diminished health, and more. When you are not living authentically, true to your nature, life feels like a constant uphill battle. Discover your authentic self with the benefit of a complete and accurate picture of the entire spectrum of your personality, ask me (Hardy@HardySmith.com) about the CORE Multidimensional Awareness Profile.

GENERAL CORE ATTRIBUTES

COMMANDER
(Column A)

Normally

- Extroverted, Assertive, Serious
- Thrives on Power and Authority
- Decisive, Matter-of-fact Relating
- Enjoys Competition, Challenge, and Purposeful Activity
- Relates to Clear-Cut Decisions and Tangible Benefits

Under Stress Becomes

- Aggressive
- Bossy/Controlling
- Impatient
- Louder
- Belligerent

ORGANIZER
(Column B)

Normally

- Introverted, Reserved, Serious
- Thrives on Order and Procedure
- Detailed – Systems Oriented
- Thorough, Cautious Relating
- Enjoys Structure, Predictability, and Factual Information
- Relates to Constancy, Planning, Accuracy, and Dependability

Under Stress Becomes

- Passive/Aggressive
- Withdrawn, Cold
- Stubborn, Resistant
- Narrow-Minded
- Silent or Sarcastic

RELATER
(Column C)

Normally

- Introverted, Reserved, Playful
- Thrives on Cooperation and Sharing
- Patient – Construction Oriented
- Friendly, Supportive Relating
- Enjoys Stability, Reassurance, and Pleasant Surroundings
- Relates to Loyalty, Flexibility, Consistency, and Duty

Under Stress Becomes

- Passive, Submissive
- Withdrawn, Hurt
- Stubborn, Sensitive
- Guilt Laden
- Silent or Tearful

ENTERTAINER
(Column D)

Normally

- Extroverted, Assertive, Playful
- Thrives on Action and Enthusiasm
- Energetic – Interaction Oriented
- Friendly, Matter-of-fact Relating
- Enjoys Spontaneity, Change, and Communicating
- Relates to Discussion, Debate, and Friendly Competition

Under Stress Becomes

- Aggressive
- Pushy/Argumentative
- Impatient
- Louder
- Demanding

STOP THE NONPROFIT BOARD BLAME GAME

	C Commander	O Organizer	R Relater	E Entertainer
General Traits	Bold Risk Taker Loves a Challenge Direct Assertive Status Conscious	Analytical Detail Oriented Practical Economical Systematic Fair	Easygoing Quiet Good Listener Hides Feelings Consistent Predictable	People Oriented Outgoing Optimistic Idealistic Emotional Friendly
Helpful Traits	Confident Ambitious Decisive Innovative Persuasive Goal Oriented Leader	Accurate Orderly Persevering Consistent Careful Stable Focused	Flexible Kind Thoughtful Helpful Patient Consistent Supportive	Enthusiastic Inspirational Cooperative Flexible Friendly Quick Wit Good Communicator
Possible Problematic Traits	Strong Willed Impatient Not Sensitive Rash Overconfident Intimidating	Cautious Slow to Change Won't Commit Procrastinates Nit-picky Critical	Indecisive Dependent Evasive Won't Open Up Strong Need to Please	Forgetful Misallocates Time Too Much Small Talk May Not Listen Won't Admit Lack of Knowledge
Needs	Action Results Accomplishment Challenge Sense of Control Efficiency Credit	Stability Logic Details & Facts Certainty Fairness Order Recognition of Skill	Reassurance Direction Guidance Constancy Stability Security Quiet Appreciation	Friendship To be Popular Freedom to Choose To be Heard Self Expression Interaction Open Appreciation
How to Relate	Be Specific, Brief, and to the Point Be Prepared Know your Stuff Sell with Action and Impact	Show Logic of Ideas Give Facts Show Proof Give Logical, Orderly Presentation Sell Value	Show Sincere Interest Provide Reassurance Stress Benefits Show Concern Help Them Decide Soft Sell	Listen Actively Compliment Sincerely Be Friendly Offer Choices Use Their Name Often Sell Emotionally

The influences shaping individual behaviors affect how people interact with others. With insights gained from the CORE Snapshot and CORE Attributes and Dimensions charts, can you more fully appreciate how better understanding your own traits and the traits of others correlates with establishing relationships on a deeper level? Understanding people and their behaviors can produce positive outcomes—among board members, as well as with others in your life. When you know whether the person you're addressing is more of a risk taker or more focused on analysis, you can then tailor your message accordingly.

Consider conducting a facilitated full personality assessment exercise. It would be a powerful activity to incorporate into an annual board retreat. But even without the benefit of a personality assessment, you can still develop a basic awareness of someone's characteristics in order to determine how to best appeal to them. You can observe how they dress and how their home or office is decorated and organized and pay attention to how they communicate to identify their personality type. There are, in fact, numerous clues that can provide you with the type of insights to know and understand people better—and to improve board relationships.

An example of personality tip-offs is communication styles. For example, communicating in a succinct delivery that's to the point with little detail could indicate a Commander personality. Sharing detailed information backed up with plenty of research data could indicate an Organizer. Showing strong listening skills and being empathetic could indicate a Relator. And projecting enthusiastic excitement for a point or points made could indicate an Entertainer.

For more hints to an individual's traits keep the CORE resource documents in mind when interacting with others.

COMMIT TO ENSURING BOARD MEMBERS
KNOW EACH OTHER

A board whose members don't truly know each other will have difficulty maximizing its potential. Chances for communication mistakes will be much more likely, and the overall board experience, critical for nurturing full engagement, may not be as positive and productive as it needs to be.

Is each of your board members able to hold a conversation on a more personal level with other board members? Do they know the backgrounds of their colleagues, what's important to them, and why their board service is meaningful to them? If the answer is no, then more get-to-know-you work is needed.

Knowing your board members matters. Board members knowing one another matters, too.

The benefit to you is a board with a positive culture that can provide your organization with dynamic leadership and guidance through collaboration, consensus, and compromise, all of which are essential for successful and productive interaction among your CEOs, board chairs, and board members.

What have been your experiences when knowing or not knowing a board member has impacted your nonprofit? What are other proactive approaches to knowing your board members you can take?

....

Develop your action steps

- How well do you know your board members?

- What activity would facilitate knowing your board members better?

- How well do your board members know each other?

- What activity would facilitate board members knowing each other better?

11

CHANGE YOUR APPROACH
TO BOARD ENGAGEMENT

Having engaged board members who are fully committed to carrying out every task is an organization's dream. Unfortunately, the reality is that dreams about board engagement are often nightmares. Expectations ranging from fundraising to executing leadership roles to participating in events frequently go unmet.

The question is "Why?" If your current approaches aren't reducing your level of frustration, it's time to either fix them or adopt new practices. The key is to accept the challenge of reevaluating your approach to board engagement. Commit to implementing strategies that will make your dream a reality.

IDENTIFY THE THREE ENGAGEMENT INFLUENCERS

Let's use information we've covered in previous chapters to find new solutions to engagement challenges, but first, let's examine three key trends influencing your ability to get that much yearned-for involvement. These influencers play a significant role in determining how successful your efforts will be.

The first is social disengagement, a national trend identified, as noted earlier, by Robert Putnam. Putnam characterizes this phenomenon as beginning in the early 1960s and affecting every type of volunteer and membership-related organization. The downward spiral of social involvement continues, and there is no indication of it reversing course.

The second major influencer is generational shift. As responsibility moves from one age group to the next, board engagement is one of many aspects of nonprofit management that will evolve.

The impact on an organization dealing with individuals representing the five different generational groups is substantial. As we mentioned earlier, seniors, baby boomers, and Gen X, Y, and Z have distinctly different behavioral characteristics. How does this shift affect the nonprofit and association world? Picture your board, and put an age with each face. You probably have representation by each generational group. The triggers that each of these groups reacts to are very different. How do you engage five distinctly different perspectives?

Although, as Putnam noted, social engagement is declining in general, don't fall for the misperception that the younger generations are doing so at a greater rate than their predecessors. They do get engaged, and they will be involved. It's just that they don't do it the way that previous generations have done it.

Here's another fallacy about generational shift and board performance influence: "Those younger people, when they get older, they'll know better. They'll be a lot smarter. They'll see it the way they're supposed to." I have news for you: It's not happening. All the research shows that whatever personality traits they exhibit today are the same they're going to exhibit in the future. If you want them engaged with your organization later, you have to attract them while they're young and bring them along. Note: Start with smart choices, not fixer-uppers.

A third influencer to consider is the effect of change represented by our growing cultural and ethnic diversification. As the nation's population evolves into one that is increasingly multicultural, greater understanding and appreciation of unique beliefs and values is vital when seeking to attract engagement. In addition, different backgrounds bring to the table new insights, new perspectives, and new approaches to dealing with age-old nonprofit and association challenges.

The results of these three influencers can be found in the annual nationwide survey on volunteering conducted by the Corporation for National and Community Service (CNCS). The CNCS (www. nationalservice.gov) report provides an in-depth statistical analysis of the country's volunteer activity. Organizations in states with a higher ranking have populations with a greater propensity for being attracted to volunteer roles, such as serving on a nonprofit board.

While the national figures are interesting, I find the state-by-state results for demographic categories to be telling—and somewhat troubling. My home state of Florida, year in and year out, consistently ranks at the bottom of all measurement indicators in the CNCS volunteering report. This finding gives valuable insight that board recruitment and retention challenges in the Sunshine State are quite daunting.

Social disengagement, generational shift, and growing cultural diversity all add to the difficulty of reaching desired levels of engagement. Heightened awareness of these challenges is critical to achieving engagement success. In fact, not taking them into full account will doom your efforts to failure. These obstacles can, however, be overcome with new approaches. If current practices aren't producing desired results, doesn't it just make sense to abandon what isn't working and adopt a positive new engagement-building process?

REPLACE INEFFECTIVE PRACTICES

Until the late 1800s, hospitals were notorious environments for widespread infection. Surgical patients in particular suffered from infections and frequently died. The standard health practices of the day are now unthinkable. The unsanitary conditions continued until Dr. Joseph Lister challenged conventional thinking and advocated the use of sterile procedures as a way to reduce infection. In the nonprofit world, disappointment in board member engagement may not cause immediate infection and death, but the consequent failure of the organization mission can cause or permit a myriad of problems ranging from miserable to life threatening.

> If current practices aren't producing desired results, doesn't it just make sense to abandon what isn't working and adopt a positive new engagement-building process?

I am advocating that you think like Lister. Try something new to solve a compelling problem. Dr. Lister's much-challenged methodology involved changing clothes worn during surgeries, washing hands, and using disinfectants to clean wounds and surgical incisions. These changes in behavior didn't involve the patients. It was the health-care professionals who had to alter their practices to achieve a different result. Rather than continue to be stressed by expecting board member behavior to change on its own, consider changing your approach to produce new results.

TAKE LEADERSHIP ACTION

The desire to move beyond the status quo must be a driving force to make transformational change happen. Altering the behavior of board members requires nonprofit leaders to first being willing to alter their own. Shifting from the familiar to something new isn't easy, but it is necessary.

With that commitment in place, here are actions that will improve board member engagement.

Rethink how expectations are set

Taking action to improve board member engagement should start with rethinking how expectations are established. Examine whether or not the organization's priorities are also the priorities of board members. Determine what the priority focus should be for board members' time.

A CHAMBER CASE STUDY

My presentation on creating engaged chamber boards to the Florida Association of Chamber Professionals provides an excellent example of expectations being out of sync with board member willingness to meet them. Prior to the presentation, I conducted a survey of those registered to attend to identify their biggest challenges with board engagement. The responses indicated the issue causing the most frustration was board members not showing up for chamber events, such as after-hours business socials and typical ceremonial activities like ribbon cuttings. This was ironic, because the chamber professionals were otherwise satisfied with board meeting attendance, participation in major activities like annual banquets, and other large-scale signature events.

To address this particular challenge, I asked the audience to characterize the makeup of a chamber board. Typically, they are key business and community leaders, which translates into extremely busy people. These are strategic thinkers who provide direction and then delegate to others for implementation. They most likely don't have hands-on involvement in every little aspect of their business.

Furthermore, their own business-related time constraints prohibit them from anytime chamber work. I suggested to the chamber professionals that their frustration could be caused by unrealistic expectations. The classic board member should be treated as a high-value asset whose time commitment is limited. An organization should prioritize how that asset can best be used.

Certainly, what's important will be different for each entity, and I admit to being somewhat biased, but does an organization's success really depend on every board member being in attendance at every nonbusiness function?

How can you resolve your desire to have board member involvement in activities that they probably wouldn't rank as very important? Consider asking your board members to commit to a rotating schedule of representation. You could also present a list of activities and ask them to select their participation preferences. Involvement from other chamber members could also help when a chamber presence is needed. This has the added benefit of previewing new potential board prospects. Finally, if an activity has a level of importance that isn't readily apparent, communicate that to board members so they will get the message that this is more than a routine request. Successful organizations put a premium on recruiting blue-chip prospects for their boards. Those talents are being negated if they're not being used appropriately.

During my aforementioned youth basketball coaching days, I got excellent guidance from Hall of Fame basketball coach Steve Ridder, of Embry Riddle Aeronautical University. His advice reinforces an overriding theme from the survey: "Make sure the right players are in the right positions." Coach Ridder's direction is very much applicable to board member engagement. Just like basketball players, board members should be paired with tasks they can and will successfully execute.

If the same engagement needs continuously go unmet, then it's likely board members do not accept them as their responsibility. Why continue to be frustrated by holding onto expectations that your board members have shown they're not going to fulfill? Is it likely they're going to change? Probably not. But *you* can.

Wouldn't it be more productive to focus board members' engagement in activities they will commit to and redirect other tasks to non-board members who may be better suited for those responsibilities? This advice could be difficult to put into practice for the smaller nonprofit where board members might be thought of as a manpower source for conducting events. When this is the case, step up volunteer recruitment in order to lessen the time demand on your board members. As with getting other general members to participate, this approach will also provide an opportunity for identifying individuals with future board service potential.

Expectations can't be unilaterally set and imposed on those who are expected to implement them.

Once again, rethinking expectations as a necessary action to improve engagement has a critically important component: Expectations can't be unilaterally set and imposed on those who are expected to implement them.

Create ownership

Inclusion is the key ingredient in the recipe for success when establishing expectations. Participation in decision-making helps create buy-in. The process that produces buy-in generates what Troy University Chancellor Dr. Jack Hawkins calls "creating ownership." That ownership translates into a vested interest in seeing a task through to completion.

As I have noted, asking rather than telling what you expect from a group of volunteers—asking for input rather than giving orders—will reinforce inclusion and reap positive benefits.

When should that communication start? Discussion of engagement expectation should be initiated in the recruiting stage. Waiting until after *I do*s are said at the altar of the board does not make for a positive relationship. Don't assume what's been agreed to in the past by previous boards will be accepted by present-day board members. As individuals transition off and onto the board, conduct, refresh, and reset exercises for expectations that meet the approval of the current board.

Taking time for individual input on engagement priorities or conducting a facilitated critical conversation with your entire board demonstrates the importance you place on board member opinion about actions they will be asked to take. Expectations should not be automatically assumed to be yours, mine, and ours, but shared ownership can be achieved with a participatory process.

Recognize an important engagement distinction

It's important to separate expectations into governance and non-governance tasks. Being all-in with governance roles isn't optional for board members. So, if participation is coming up short, that's a major problem. It must be dealt with, not left to fester as a tolerated source of irritation. Waiting for a term to expire may be the easy way out, but allowing nonperformance to persist impacts the mission, not to mention the morale of dedicated members.

Direct interaction is required. Individuals must realize that failure to perform puts not only themselves but also the organization at risk. Once requirements for governance engagement are clearly explained, disengaged board members have the choice of accepting their legal duty or withdrawing from the board. Sometimes, tougher action may be necessary to protect the organization, and you must remove someone unwilling to comply with the required governance involvement. There is an organizational responsibility to ensure safe governance practices in the boardroom are followed.

Reinforce expectations

Reinforcement of expectations should be ongoing so that awareness of important tasks remains front and center. Keep expectations top of mind with orientations, training sessions, board meetings, and individual discussion.

Reward the behavior you want. That recognition will serve to keep engaged board members motivated and will also encourage others to get engaged with activities they might not have otherwise been willing to do.

Recruit with focus on engagement

Recruiting the wrong people obviously creates engagement issues. Avoid this situation by asking the right board prospects to join your board.

Here are three practices that can eliminate recruiting mistakes that create self-inflicted damage to board member engagement. Let's reframe the recruiting strategies we discussed earlier to the perspective of increasing board engagement.

Don't buy into the busy person myth

How frequently do we hear "If you want something done, ask a busy person?" And each time we nod knowingly as if that is some great wisdom handed down from an all-knowing leadership guru.

Be realistic. The reality is that going after busy people because they get things done can be counterproductive. How many number-one priorities can someone realistically have? And are you willing to be less than a top priority?

Rethink this myth. If a person is involved in multiple organizations, how many board meetings can they reasonably attend? How many charitable dinners can they go to? How many donation checks will they write? How many times will their friends accept their fundraising solicitation calls? Bottom line, how many causes can be their most important priority?

Consider the infamous elevator speech. Almost all board engagement training sessions include encouragement for each board member to have a thirty-second elevator speech ready to deliver. However, imagine this: At the business after-hours event, an enthusiastic board member strikes up a conversation and dutifully works in an elevator speech. As the brief interaction is concluded and just before the other party moves to walk away, our board member says, "Wait, I have five more elevator speeches to share."

Which of your board members' half dozen elevator speeches will they be sharing? Will it be yours? The right person for you may not be the busy person. If you want someone who is focused on your singular organization, consider not going after individuals who serve on several other boards.

Of course, there are exceptions. The individual who does have plenty of time and is willing to divide it equally among different causes can still be an effective board member and champion of your cause.

Think creatively. Work just a little harder to identify people with greater flexibility with their scheduling commitments and a passion for your cause in their hearts.

Don't assume

Don't assume that your expectations are understood by others. Don't assume that your expectations hold the same level of importance with all board members either. Don't assume that individuals who don't have needed experience, skill sets, or time can be converted into high-performance or even adequate board members.

Know your board prospects

My study of personality characteristics shows me that each individual's persona greatly determines what type of board member they will be. Take into account that personality traits directly impact how individuals process information. The greater personality diversity on your board, the more work required to ensure each individual receives your communication in a positive way. Yes, this takes extra effort, but it is necessary and certainly pays off both now and in the long run.

Knowing your board members makes a difference. Let's look again at Bill France Jr. and his type-A communication style. When I worked for him, I can guarantee you that his communication preference was to be brief and to the point: "Hardy, just tell me if it's raining. I don't need a full weather report." As long as I followed his preference for receiving information, I had his attention. If he asked for more background, it was okay to go into greater detail.

If you want board members to be fundraisers, get fundraisers. Not everyone is willing to ask others for money. Assuming nonfundraisers will behave differently because they are board members is just asking to be frustrated.

As we discussed, a no from a prospect can be the best answer for all concerned.

Improve communication to improve engagement

It's unreasonable to expect engagement without effective communication. Effective communication directly elevates engagement. The more informative it is, the more engaged board members will be.

Often, despite a communicated need for involvement, expected participation doesn't happen. If you find yourself in this situation, evaluate whether or not communication methods are a contributing factor. For example, when discussing engagement expectations with board prospects, don't assume that a one-and-done conversation will provide a complete understanding about their role in the organization. In order to realistically expect them to meet the desired performance level, you must confirm their acceptance and commitment. That confirmation also sets the stage for accountability.

Communicate for results

You sent out promotional material. You mentioned an event at the board meeting. And you're puzzled because participation response isn't what you hoped for. How often at a board meeting is there a need-to-be-there calendar passed out accompanied with the familiar "Here's our schedule, and it sure would be good to have all of our board members in attendance"? Then what happens? The activities are held, and frustration (or worse) sets in because board members don't show up.

To get the results you intend, make sure that your volunteers know that their time will have an impact. You have to tell it—compellingly—in order to sell it. Be clear about the level of importance of a particular activity. Getting engagement takes more than just sending out a single piece of information or giving a brief announcement about an upcoming activity. Make communication efforts commensurate with how badly you want your board members engaged with a certain activity.

Be careful, though, to be judicious with pushing for involvement because there can be only so many top requests that someone will respond to. Scale your involvement appeals accordingly. When a full board presence is needed, communicate that. However, if only a few board representatives will suffice, concentrate on individual asks. When working to build participation commitment, help busy individuals understand the relevance of the task in the scheme of your organization's mission. Communicate what their attendance will help accomplish.

I groan every time someone says they are passing a sign-up list around. Rarely have I ever seen that get the people needed. You can start with a list, because folks just may indicate they will play a part. But don't leave it there. Each activity should have a participation goal associated with it. If the list pass-around doesn't get the required numbers, individual calls from you, the event chair, or board chair will convey importance. And don't stop the sign-up push when enough confirmations are reached. Get a few extras to account for no-shows.

After people do commit to participate, follow up with reminders. Let them know in advance how much their involvement is appreciated. And always, always thank them afterward.

Make a proper ask to secure engagement

Regardless of the task, proper communication structure of an ask will go a long way toward a successful request for the individual's engagement. The appropriate approach when asking someone to take on a specific role will be much more likely to result in confirmed acceptance of the work to be done and will establish accountability for fulfilling the personal performance commitment that has been made.

Communicate the importance of the assignment, provide specifics about what is expected, and outline a time line for accomplishing the task. Conduct this process within the framework of a two-way dialogue. A prerequisite is to prequalify the subject of your ask. Do the necessary homework to ensure the individual can reasonably be expected to get the job done. Set up the conversation by requesting an appointment to discuss an item of importance. This projects seriousness and shows recognition that their time is valuable.

The purpose of the conversation is to establish understanding of the task, answer questions, and address concerns. It may also reveal constraints on the individual's ability to achieve the goal that weren't previously known such as a change in work schedules, family commitments, or health situations. In that case, do not pressure someone into a yes.

AN EXAMPLE FOR MAKING THE ASK

Elizabeth, our leadership believes you are the ideal person to head up sponsorship solicitation for our signature fundraising event. You have demonstrated the ability for successfully delivering financial support in the past, and we feel others will follow your lead as the chair.

The goal is to raise $250,000, which will generate a net profit of $200,000 after event expenses. All sponsorships should be secured three months prior to the event so we know our finances are in order and so the sponsors can get good pre-event publicity.

Is this a responsibility you feel comfortable taking on?

Following this individualized approach has a psychological benefit. It projects confidence in the individual and appeals to their own sense of self-esteem. Acceptance of a task presented in this manner creates a platform for an essential element when working with volunteers—the follow-up.

With volunteers you will get what you follow up on.

MAKE MEETINGS MATTER

Research on meeting productivity reveals that leaders are spending increasing amounts of time in meetings. The research also reveals that the majority of time devoted to meetings is viewed as unproductive. My own research into nonprofit board performance issues has found that, when board members feel their time is being wasted, they become disengaged.

Facing the cold, hard facts, how would you evaluate the effectiveness of your meetings? Do they turn on—or turn off—the participants? Are your meetings disorganized or poorly run? Do they have little compelling purpose? Do they fail to encourage active discussion? Volunteers want their opinions to be valued and the investment of their time to result in positive outcomes.

Here are two signs that your meetings are perceived as ineffective. First, you have poor attendance. Second, those who do show up don't participate well because they are not prepared. They haven't reviewed meeting materials in advance because the meeting isn't important enough to them to invest more time than they already are by attending.

Make your board meetings matter by implementing these five tips:

- Ensure that meetings are well planned and that the chair is prepared.

- Structure agendas so that time is devoted to priority topics, such as the status of a strategic goal or a challenge that board insight could help resolve.

- Welcome dialogue and questions. Encourage the use of facilitation techniques by the meeting chair to ensure that everyone participates. Provide chairs with facilitator training if needed.

- Allow for social interaction either before or after meetings. Everyone likes opportunities to socialize, and this important activity helps reinforce personal connections. Among volunteers, these relationships are often the reason they stay engaged with their board service.

- Solicit board member suggestions for how to improve meetings so that they stimulate excitement.

Making your meetings matter will motivate board members to attend. They will know that their time is being respected, their opinions are being considered, and their commitment is producing worthwhile outcomes.

What other ideas do you have for making sure board meetings are motivating for participants and producing positive results?

TAKE ACTION TO IMPROVE ENGAGEMENT

Frustration with board member engagement may never be totally eliminated, but it can be greatly reduced by following these suggestions:

- Recognize the three engagement influencers
- Rethink how expectations are set
- Recruit with focus on engagement
- Refine communication to improve engagement

Volunteer engagement cannot be demanded. It requires thoughtful attention to details relating to interpersonal relationships. When expectations are realistic and prioritized and have buy-in, they are much more likely to be met. While each board member represents unique challenges to stimulating individual involvement, consider changes that you, as a staff or board leader, may need to make to improve your communication skills and interaction effectiveness.

Is it time for change? Consider: Would your mission benefit from reworking the structure of the model for how you establish expectations, who you would recruit to execute those expectations, or how you approach those being asked to carry out tasks important to your organization? Joseph Lister created changes in public health behavior and expectations. Likewise, you can create positive change in your social sector by rethinking your approach to board member engagement.

....

Develop your action steps

- What specific areas of board member engagement need improving?

- What engagement expectations should be reevaluated?

- How can board members' time be better used?

- What communication practices should be initiated to help improve engagement?

12

MAKE BOARD
DIVERSITY WORK

Board members who represent the many diverse communities can become frustrated when there is a lack of full-on organizational commitment to diversity. Adopting a goal to achieve diversity is one thing. Taking action to be successful is quite another.

Despite ongoing encouragement for nonprofit boards to embrace diversity, research shows that even moderate movement toward more diverse boards is just not happening on a broad scale. The natural consequences are that individuals from underrepresented groups become frustrated, discouraged, and disengaged from their board service.

Organizations whose commitment to diversity is not demonstrable and active send a clear signal that it isn't a priority. This message projects well beyond the boardroom to prospective board members, members, volunteers, staff, and donors. These organizations

> **Adopting a goal to achieve diversity is one thing. Taking action to be successful is quite another.**

are shooting themselves in the foot: Their negative reputation will drive away individuals they would like—and need—to attract.

COMMIT TO BOARD DIVERSITY

My speaker colleague Dr. Shirley Davis is a recognized global workforce expert and specializes in diversity and inclusion. I asked her for guidance she would like to share. She advises, "Any conversation around achieving organizational diversity should not be narrowly focused on just gender and race. True diversity isn't about quotas."

Dr. Davis notes that organizations will benefit from recognizing critical perspective. "Optics matter. When an individual doesn't see anyone else who looks like them, it communicates that their values and needs aren't important."

She recommends these actions for successfully implementing a goal for achieving board diversity:

- Recognize that there can be unconscious biases that prevent action from being taken.

- Identify a champion to lead the initiative.

- Develop a positioning statement that covers what the organization believes and that defines what is to be accomplished.

- Establish goals with measurable outcomes.

- Evaluate progress being made.

- Provide training and facilitated discussion that gives your goal a top-of-mind presence.

Avoid mistakes that will block implementation success. Dr. Davis identifies these four as especially significant.

- Failing to see that achieving diversity goals is everyone's responsibility

- Failing to recognize that there can be diversity and not inclusion

- Failing to foster assimilation so that there is a sense of belonging

- Assuming that achieving diversity is a quick thing— it's a marathon, not a sprint

To create a true culture of diversity, Dr. Davis advocates going beyond focus on just the board by "operationalizing" your efforts. Consider leadership positions, committee involvement, program scheduling, employee hiring, vendor selection, member and volunteer recruitment, and donor acquisition as opportunities for achieving organizational diversity.

Further demonstrate your commitment to diversity by ensuring that the public view of your organization, such as through your website and social media activity, includes leadership statements that reflect on various aspects of diversity.

RECRUIT TO ACHIEVE DIVERSITY

As I mentioned, there is a wide gap between organizations that claim commitment to diversity and those that actually take action steps in that direction. What is missing is either appropriately targeted recruiting or a recruiting process that works.

To help find solutions for nonprofits that want to overcome recruiting obstacles, I turned to Jim Taylor, vice president for leadership initiatives at BoardSource. Jim's personal and professional background make him an ideal board candidate. His willingness to share his lived experience as a person of color recruited for board service provides valuable insight. His perspective helps create awareness that many organizations may not have. This lack of awareness contributes to missing the mark on diversity recruiting and the critical inclusionary actions that must follow.

I asked him to help nonprofit leaders gain a greater understanding of the underlying issues that affect diversity-related recruiting. I also requested that he identify how-to actions that will lead to positive recruiting results. Most importantly, I wanted him to share steps organizations should take to create a culture of inclusion after recruitment goals seem to have been met.

Jim's first advice is to encourage boards to have a purpose or policy statement that guides their diversity and inclusion initiative. He then recommends this BoardSource resource: "Taking Action on Board Diversity: Five Questions to Get You Started." It is available on the BoardSource website, BoardSource.org.

"Be intentional about recruiting," Jim advises. "Board and staff retreats should include conversation on why board diversity matters—diversity in terms of cultural and ethnic background, skills, areas of expertise, and lived experiences."

Jim offers these specific recruiting strategies for nonprofits wanting to develop a more diverse board. These how-tos are excellent for organizations that say their efforts are stalled because "they don't know anyone." Build on these suggestions by recruiting with purpose and process, as we discussed earlier.

Change your current approach by recruiting differently. Grow your pool of prospects by going outside of your board members' everyday circles. Identify board candidates beyond the usual go-to individuals that seem to be most visible and most frequently asked.

Reach individuals listed on diverse databases by posting board openings on Internet sites such as DiversityJobs.com or the Black Career Network. Contact national organizations such as the National Black Chamber of Commerce, the National Black MBA Association, or the Hispanic National Bar Association for local connections in your area that you can network with. The more visible an organization is with efforts like this, the more it demonstrates their willingness to take extra steps. This is a message that will get favorable attention from those you are trying to recruit.

Enlist your staff in prospecting efforts. They are out in the field every day and likely know people who would be good fits for your board. They will probably be aware of young emerging leaders who aren't yet on anyone else's radar.

Identify other stakeholders serving the same mission emphasis and seek out relationships that could lead to new board members. In the business sector, discover which corporations have social responsibility priorities that match your service purpose, and inquire about a company-supported addition to your board.

Recruit to your mission. Seek out individuals with a passion for your cause and ask them for referrals.

Use your volunteer program to expand diversification. Growing the number of diverse volunteers not only strengthens your community connections; it gives you a source for potential future board members.

Conduct a recruiting debrief with each new board member. Ask them to share how the process went for them, what might be improved, and what—if anything—might have caused them to hesitate on accepting your invitation.

AVOID MISTAKES WITH PROSPECTS

Jim is aware of how recruitment efforts can be mishandled. He feels the following situation he experienced is not an uncommon one. How do you think Jim, as a person of color, responded to an invitation to join a board when it was clear, first, that the invitation was because of race, then, that the organization didn't consider his qualifications, and finally, that there were no expectations beyond filling a board seat?

He said no thank you. And the organization lost the opportunity to add a terrific new board member.

He says, "Race should not be the only lens that boards apply to their search. Boards that focus on race as the sole qualification for board membership are employing an overly simplistic approach that is disrespectful to the people of color they are recruiting. Boards should be applying multiple lenses as they consider their needs; racial identity should be a part of that consideration—but not all of it."

Board recruiters should be aware that individuals representing diverse populations are listening carefully to find out if an invitation is being extended because someone has the perfect qualifications or because they're being used to merely check a box. Recognize this sensitivity and strengthen your invitation by referring to specific contributions that you see the individual being able to make.

CREATE A CULTURE OF INCLUSION

Jim agrees with Dr. Davis on the significance of inclusion: Inclusion is how the concept of diversity is implemented. Inclusion creates a sense of belonging and determines how an individual will feel about their experience. A board position that doesn't include inclusive involvement will be a source of frustration—a negative situation that, in fact, creates exclusion.

"I especially want to emphasize this point. If I am the only person of color on the board, I get concerned if the board's first question to me regarding diversifying the board is, 'Who else do you know?' I will certainly help, but what I really want to see is *every* board member being involved. I want to know that every board member is asking themselves how they can be a stronger diversity advocate. That's how you build a culture of inclusion."

To get a new board member off to a good start, Jim recommends that the organization be quick in providing a detailed orientation and also support them with a mentor or a board buddy. He further urges, "They should be engaged in the work right away, such as immediate assignment to committees. That sends the message that they're not just filling a seat."

Another area that Jim brings attention to is that of social inclusion. "It is important to think about social practices that involve board members. For example, what happens if there is a regularly scheduled time when board members get together socially and a new member has a standing conflict with that date and is unable to attend? Being mindful that individuals bring different life situations to a group will help demonstrate there is a willingness to make accommodations so everyone can participate."

Use diversity and inclusion as a strategy to not only better represent your community but as a way to strengthen your organization and your board. A board culture that is welcoming and inclusive will help attract and retain individuals representing diverse demographics. It's important to recognize that opening up consciousness and developing pathways that lead to diversity success takes time and commitment to do the work necessary.

He adds, "In the context of a board setting, what I'm looking for is a culture of candor, trust, and respect. A place where everyone on the board feels heard and valued."

As nonprofits take action on their commitment to board diversity and inclusion, following the advice of Dr. Davis and Jim Taylor will help remove a source of frustration among diverse board members. This guidance will also help organizations position themselves as much more attractive to individuals representing different races, cultures, genders, and generational groups.

Does your organization have a goal for increasing diversity and for creating intentional inclusion? What actions are you taking to achieve your goal?

....

Develop your action steps

- What are your organization's priorities for diversity?

- What actions are needed to support your diversity priorities?

- How can your diversity recruitment efforts be improved?

- What practices will you implement to ensure your diversity goals have a focus on inclusion?

13

COMMUNICATE EFFECTIVELY

The value of communicating effectively cannot be overstated. When I ask audiences what they believe is the most essential element of any successful long-term relationship, they consistently cite good communication. More specifically, board members participating in my research said that poor communication is a major pain point that creates many unnecessary issues affecting board and organization success. It's the domino effect. Inattention leads to poor messaging. Poor messaging leads to diminished board experience. Diminished board experience leads to poor board performance.

Nonprofit leaders who want better relationships with—and performance from—their board members can start by focusing on being good communicators. Let's identify specific obstacles that can affect good communication and look at solutions to overcome them. When you maintain a higher level of effectiveness for board communication, you will strengthen board relationships and board performance.

DON'T TREAT YOUR BOARD MEMBERS
LIKE MUSHROOMS

Board members have shared with me examples of poor communication—for instance, flawed timing, a lack of information, and not being listened to. The frustration they experience can lead to feelings of being misled—or worse.

Does communication with your board members leave them feeling like mushrooms—kept in the dark and covered with manure?

Make no mistake; such feelings affect trust. Board members can feel like mushrooms in a grow house—kept in the dark and covered with manure. It's unreasonable to expect them to work cooperatively with someone they don't feel positive about or whose reliability they question.

Keep your board members informed in a timely and honest fashion. Even if the root of the problem is unintentional, they must be able to trust that you are supplying the tools they need to succeed.

RECOGNIZE THE SIGNIFICANCE OF
QUALITY MESSAGING

You may feel the frequency of your contacts with board members is more than adequate. But does an impressive level of activity mean that the contacts are effective? While frequency is, indeed, important, quantity doesn't automatically translate into quality.

Yes, you send minutes, reports, financials, and the rest. But don't assume that board members fully understand all the information you send. The more training opportunities and background information you can offer, the more involved they will become and the more competent they will be.

If your board members are not responding with desired results, consider the quality of your communication techniques. Thinking of all of the communications you have with board members, are they contributing to positive performance outcomes or inadvertently adding to the frustration of expectations not being met? Communication efforts need to incorporate appropriate quantity *and* quality to be effective.

MAKE FIRST OPPORTUNITIES COUNT

A common first communication transgression occurs during recruitment when, as mentioned earlier, a full explanation of duties is omitted in eagerness to get a yes from a board prospect. For example, board members who find out later about time commitments and fundraising expectations feel misled.

The second chance for establishing good communications is during a new board member's orientation. Yet many organizations fail to capitalize on this opportunity. In fact, poorly done or ineffective orientations are a reason that a solid foundation for communications and positive relationships are lost.

Research from BoardSource offers proof that early interactions with board members are not delivering the results they should. According to their study, staff is critical of board members' lack of awareness of their responsibilities.

Isn't the organization responsible for disseminating information about board member roles and responsibilities? First-impression opportunities are critical. If recruitment and orientation are mishandled, chances for a positive bond are already compromised.

TAKE TIPS FROM A TOP COMMUNICATOR

Reading *What More Can I Say?* by communication expert Dianna Booher helped me appreciate the fundamentals that go into being a successful communicator. Nonprofit leaders who want to up their game should follow two important tips from Dianna.

Her first tip is to "listen for what's *not* said in a conversation or document. Why did the person *not* mention a particular topic? Why did the person not ask the next logical question? Why did the person skirt an issue when it would have been typical and reasonable to discuss the topic? Their silence speaks volumes. Probe for under-the-surface information, feelings, or motivations to fully understand a situation."

Dianna's second tip deals with the big communication mistake of "failing to listen discriminately." She suggests, "probing with questions to help draw accurate conclusions so you can make sound decisions."

These words of advice have another critical function. They reveal how board members are judging the messages they're receiving.

Adapt communications to reach different generations

Communicating successfully includes a variety of issues that are vital to nonprofits. There are donors to reach, volunteers to recruit, causes to publicize, and program participants to sign up. Basic to ensuring that outreach efforts are being executed with maximum effectiveness is making certain that vital messages are clearly identified and, more importantly, understood. This is becoming increasingly difficult because of one of the most significant changes affecting communications today: the generational shift I mentioned earlier.

Recognizing this messaging fact of life is easy. Dealing with it, not so much. Careful attention to this transition greatly enhances how effective an organization will be in reaching its communication objectives. Moreover, the impact of demographic shift will be even more dramatic as years go by. This transformation means a one-size-fits-all approach that may have been effective in the past will no longer produce the same results.

Likewise, methods an organization could previously count on for message delivery can no longer be depended on as single or even primary sources of information. Case in point: Newspapers and other print media, once a main source of information, are facing declining circulation and are now working to establish a presence on the Internet. Similarly, as viewership drops, television is using social media to build viewer connection.

To help nonprofits gain a better understanding of this change and how to cope with it, I turned to Anne Loehr who has been called the "Generational Guru" by *The Washington Post*.

As I mentioned earlier we are now a population that is made up of five generations, each of which has very different personality traits that affect preferences for receiving, processing, and responding to information. As you probably remember, the five generations are seniors, baby boomers, and Generations X, Y, and Z. Their values are different. How they choose to engage socially is different. How they communicate is different. How they process information is different.

Anne warns, "Communicating successfully with one message using a single method of delivery to all five groups is nearly impossible." To overcome the challenge this generational distinctiveness presents, Anne offers these four suggestions.

First, nonprofits will be well advised to spend more time

crafting their message. Go deep to understand your various audience targets. The more you know about who you are trying to reach, the better focused you can be.

If an organization's target is large and diverse, successful outreach may require developing multiple messaging formats for delivery through multiple communication channels. This practice applies to both board prospects and board members. Putting information into spreadsheets and charts for some people and into stories and pictures for others obviously takes more effort, but the results are well worth it.

Even though your focus presently may be on seniors and baby boomers, it is important not to discount the younger groups. The personality traits of those in the engagement pipeline for replacing today's volunteers and donors indicate building relationships with these individuals takes time, even years. Since connecting with them takes much longer than with previous generations, unless you reach them at an early age, they are likely to be committed elsewhere, and your chances for engaging them later will be lost.

Finally, it is a mistake to assume that younger generations will change their social engagement-related behavior with age. Research shows that people will carry their generational characteristics with them.

Take these suggestions from Generational Guru Anne Loehr as thought starters for strategic communication planning.

Reaching different generational groups is more than just separating your contact lists. Message content makes a difference, including choice and number of words. The various uses of graphics, video, colors, numbers, and photos also influence the effectiveness of messages within each age group. When preparing annual appeals, annual reports, event invitations, newsletters, and advertisements, and organizing plans to publicize services, think about who your intended audience is, and identify the best vehicles for reaching each of them.

Dealing effectively with generational change is a significant challenge in the evolving nonprofit world. Anne's advice on understanding the dynamics of generational differences will become increasingly important.

USE DIVERSE MESSAGING TECHNIQUES
TO ENGAGE DIVERSE MEMBERS

Yes, the substantial number of social media platforms and other forms of electronic communication are now entrenched in our lives. But there are people who for whatever reason do not keep up with all the technological advances. This fact does not affect their value as board members.

Organizations that are early adopters of new technology to the exclusion of forms previously used to connect with board members may be making a mistake—one that could create barriers instead of building bridges to successful communication. It's important to remember that individuals accept the use of new information distribution channels on their own timetables. Professional speaker Monica Wofford often talks about staying on task and not being distracted by "shiny objects" and "squirrels." While working to implement your communication strategies, don't let these new options be shiny objects that draw you away from your tried-and-true communication methods.

Make use of social media and other electronic tools to strengthen your current forms of communication. However, do not think of communication methods as an either/or choice.

Ensure your organization is communicating effectively by not autonomously deciding on a complete change in communication techniques. Write people off as inconvenient to communicate with at your own peril.

Identify the communication preferences of your individual board members. One way to show how much you value their involvement would be to ask them during initial onboarding activities how they would like to be communicated with.

KNOW THE DIFFERENCE BETWEEN ASKING AND TELLING

I was intently watching television one evening when my concentration was suddenly interrupted by an order from my wife.

"I said, 'Take out the trash!'"

I was startled for two reasons. First, my normally good-natured wife rarely uses that tone of voice. Second, I couldn't recall any earlier notice signaling the urgent importance of this chore.

"Did I miss a 'Honey, please take out the trash'?" I asked.

"No," she laughed, "I'm just in a hurry to get things done, and I was afraid that you'd just put it off if I asked nicely, so I went straight to what would get your attention. Why waste time?" Why, indeed.

How are you communicating requests for needed action to your board members? Are you asking, or are you telling? Your approach makes a tremendous difference. They are, after all, volunteers. Communication perceived as a demand will not be received in a positive way, especially by those who are giving their time freely.

Showing politeness and respect will get much better results. "Please" and "thank you" still work. A blunt and more direct communication delivery might be simpler but may hurt you—in fact, having the opposite effect from what you intend.

Positive communication is the basis for good relationships. If your communications style is creating a negative experience for your board members, what type of relationship are you building with those whose performance you are depending on?

Sure, you may be communicating, but are you communicating effectively?

Taking out the trash was a necessity, but I would have felt better about doing it if I had been asked nicely!

SEVEN MORE TIPS TO TURN COMMUNICATIONS FROM POOR TO POSITIVE

Quick reference points are always helpful. Here are seven specific actions for turning communication from poor to positive and improving relationships with board members:

Appreciate the busy schedules of your board members. Your messages are competing for attention with their overloaded in-boxes, mailboxes, and voice mails. Demonstrate that you will be communicating important information in a concise, well written manner. Your chances for consistently getting their attention will be greatly enhanced.

Don't wait until the last minute to address issues. Scheduled messages, whether written or verbal, presented in an organized, unrushed manner will be much more effective.

Advanced planning also helps avoid the pressures of deadlines, helps generate higher quality, and makes for more efficient use of time.

Schedule the release of information to allow enough time

before meetings for digesting important material. Advanced distribution is an important way to show consideration for board members' busy schedules.

Stay on top of contact information. It sounds simple, but keeping lists updated is easy to put off. Pay attention to newsletter and email bounces. I've known several prominent board members whose communication links with the organization they served were broken, and neither party was aware of it.

Appreciate the value of in-person communication. Often, email, printed materials, reports presented to a group, and even telephone calls don't have the same impact as a one-on-one, face-to-face conversation.

Be aware of physical and psychological influences when interacting with others. Your body language, tone of voice, and choice of words all matter. So do theirs. When they answer, pay attention to their body language, tone of voice, and choice of words, all of which convey what they are thinking. Understand also that individual personality and cultural differences directly influence how your message is interpreted.

COMMUNICATE IN PERSON: A PROBLEM SOLVER

Direct communication can often be best for producing the desired results.

Talladega Superspeedway is a massive facility located on several thousand acres, and its NASCAR races are among the country's largest spectator events. Its size, layout, and huge crowds make organizational logistics an enormous operational challenge. Consistently clear, concise, and broadly disseminated traffic information is not optional. Getting race fans off the highways, parked, and to their seats on time is absolutely essential to produce an exceptional customer experience.

While working as the speedway's director of administration, I was on hand for new Talladega president Mike Helton's first race. With race week rapidly approaching, Mike was faced with finding a solution to an escalating and somewhat puzzling problem. The dilemma centered around traffic backups, disorganized parking, and admission gates that were not ready to open on time. Obviously, this was not an acceptable situation.

When approached individually about any particular challenge, none of those involved with event organization seemed to have an answer except that it was someone else's fault or someone else's responsibility.

Mike's strategy for finding a resolution involved doing something not previously done. He called everyone together for some direct communication. Mike used the team approach to identify the causes of their problems and to collaboratively work out the actions that needed to be taken.

Having everyone in the same room and communicating face-to-face produced an amazing discovery. Members of the operational team really didn't know each other! Getting everyone together to communicate in person created a synergistic environment.

The dialogue helped establish positive working relationships that led to increased cooperation among the group. Everyone came to realize that they were not working in isolation. They saw how each aspect of event operations influenced the ability of others to successfully execute their responsibilities. By taking ownership for an overall result, the individuals found they could each contribute to a successful event by implementing changes that would remove obstacles from someone else. Working as a team, they found out, made everyone's tasks much easier.

Creating the opportunity for communication produced the desired result. The speedway's pre-event gridlock was eliminated. It sounds simple, but it is a valuable lesson for any organization. Ensuring effective communication, which includes the concept of interdependence, produces many positive benefits. It can solve—and prevent—a lot of pesky and avoidable problems.

Your nonprofit organization may not manage hundreds of thousands of people, but it will surely benefit from effective communication.

IMPROVE COMMUNICATION SKILLS:
AN ONGOING PROCESS

Effective communication takes commitment to a process that includes constantly seeking improvement to both technique and methodology of message delivery. The range of examples that board members cited regarding dissatisfaction with staff communication—and staffs cited regarding board member performance—is an indication that this critical foundation for relationships merits regular reassessment. This is true whether you are recruiting prospects, having the money talk, respecting your board members' volunteer status, or the innumerable other contexts of communications.

Being a good communicator will improve your leadership effectiveness, enhance relationships with board members, and, best of all, increase overall performance of your board—and your organization.

Board members are not mushrooms. Do your part to enable

them to perform as you want them to. Keep them well informed and treat them with respect.

....

Develop your action steps

- How can you evaluate your communications activity to determine its effectiveness?

- What different communication approaches should you consider initiating?

- What current communication practices should you change or eliminate?

- How can you be a better communicator?

PART 4

Adapt to Meet New Challenges

14

CHANGE BOARD
PERFORMANCE CULTURE

Provide guidance for board direction with a meaningful mission statement. A board's performance expectation should be aligned with its organization's mission statement. A compelling and concisely written mission statement provides an organization with purpose-focused guidance. A wordy or vague mission statement offers no sense of identity and no clear direction for the organization to follow. Here's a quick test to evaluate how effective your mission statement is: *Can you repeat yours right now?*

Who you are, what you do, and why you do it are the essential elements that should be communicated clearly. If it has been a while since your mission statement was reviewed, consider conducting an exercise that examines if it is still relevant or if some revision is needed. Whether updating an existing mission statement or writing a new one, seek input from key stakeholders. An inclusive approach helps develop commitment to the finished product. Do comparison shopping and check mission statements of other organizations for examples to stimulate your thoughts. Avoid trying to craft a message that appeases everyone.

A mission statement should be clear and succinct, offer a sense of identity, and clear direction. Be sure your organization has a meaningful mission statement—one that inspires volunteers, donors, members, staff, and board members alike. In addition, it should accurately reflect your purpose to the public. A solid mission statement is an anchor that guides all board action. It is also a foundation that board development should be built on.

ACCEPT THAT CHANGING CULTURE ISN'T EASY

Adapting to meet new challenges requires adopting new behaviors. But achieving acceptance of deviation from current practices can be difficult.

Convincing individuals to move in a new direction challenges the comfort of familiarity. Uncertainty of the unknown can conjure up seemingly insurmountable obstacles, even when change is necessary. Let's look at the steps to enhance your culture, performance, and engagement.

Remember Michael Gary Scott? With his personal finances spinning out of control, Steve Carell's character in the television series *The Office* gathered everyone around and announced, "I declare bankruptcy!" His coworkers then explained that using bankruptcy as a path to deal with financial difficulties involved more than a simple announcement.

Changing board culture can be complex. A successful transformation takes time and commitment.

Changing board performance culture is also much more complex than simply announcing to board members,

"I declare a new culture!" A successful transformation takes time and commitment. Here are five steps to make your board revitalization happen.

Identify the need and the course of action

To implement a culture change, establish a clear understanding of why a shift is necessary. Is there a performance expectation not being met? Is a new level of individual engagement needed?

Also essential is an explanation of the precise action required. Merely stating "You must do more" or "You must work harder" won't provide defined direction, much less enthusiastic buy-in.

In addition, communicating a clear vision of positive outcomes is critical, along with the companion piece of a clear vision of the consequences of not moving in a new direction.

Expect resistance

Resistance to a new course of action should not be a surprise. For illustrating resistance to change, I enjoy telling the story of a rare cold day in Florida—our family's first cold weather experience since moving to the Sunshine State.

To make sure our then six-year-old son was properly attired for the cold weather, my wife told him he would need to wear long pants to school the next day instead of his usual T-shirt and shorts—like he and everyone else had been wearing.

His reaction was emphatic. "No, I can't wear long pants!" The anxiety of looking different from the other children caused him to literally cry all night and even in the morning on our drive to school.

When we reached the school entrance, the look of shock on his tear-stained face was priceless. All the other children were wearing hats, gloves, coats, and, of course, long pants.

"Dad, how did she know?" he asked. "How did Mom know about the pants?"

"She's a mom, son, and moms know everything."

Why is there resistance to change? Because egos and emotions are involved. For example, change can trigger fear of the unknown. Even though the benefits of an innovative solution may appear obvious, full acceptance from stakeholders is often not automatic. Because not all board members will support moving from the comfort of long-standing practices, recognize and respect the personalities involved and devote the time necessary to gain their support. Springing surprise announcements on them could easily result in negative reactions that end your culture-enhancing initiative.

Overcome opposition

Help overcome opposition from those who are uncertain about your proposed deviation by applying steps recommended by change experts.

According to brothers Chip and Dan Heath, authors of *Switch: How to Change When Change Is Hard*, many people avoid taking action or supporting proposed change because the challenge appears overwhelming. The remedy, the Heath brothers suggest, is the incremental approach. Small steps are more easily accepted as doable, and that helps build buy-in.

Julie Henry, an expert on change and a speaker colleague of mine, has practical advice that will help nonprofits successfully execute needed change. "Change is always challenging for people, especially when it is not their idea in the first place. To successfully influence change (and make it stick), you must break it down so that people can easily understand and implement."

Julie has a three-step formula for successfully getting others to accept a new course of action.

Make it easy

Break down the change you are suggesting into steps that can be easily followed. If barriers arise or people don't understand what to do next, they will stop changing altogether. And remember, the best judges of whether or not your step-by-step action steps are easy to follow is them, not you.

Make it rewarding

People change because they see what's in it for them. They understand that if they invest their time, talent, and treasure, they will be better off.

Make it normal

People must see others like themselves already exhibiting the change you're advocating. This is the secret to influencing lasting change. If people feel like they will fit in if they make this change, they will support the change.

Change doesn't have to be chaotic. With a strategy that is incremental, valuable, and accepted, collaboration will produce positive results.

Reinforce awareness of what they're playing for

No doubt, nonprofit board members feel their service is important. But participating in board meetings, raising money, and attending events doesn't automatically translate into truly *feeling* the mission.

In his book *Great Teams*, author Don Yaeger shares the story of how the once underperforming USA basketball team returned to its preeminent position. According to Don, Duke basketball coach Mike Krzyzewski knew talent wasn't an issue when he was tapped to take over the team. He believed that the real problem was that the players had lost their focus on the importance of what they were doing. As a result, they stopped giving the effort necessary for playing like world champions.

Coach K's course of action was to create "feel-it moments." He explained, "You can try to tell people why what they do matters. You can try to show them. But people get what it means when they can feel it."

His "feel-it moments" emphasized patriotism and placing service above self. They included interaction with troops on United States military bases and an especially poignant visit to Arlington National Cemetery. The players responded with new energy and determination. Their performance level reflected a renewed spirit of pride in representing their country.

To build support for a higher level of performance, what "feel-it moments" can you create for board members that provide them with a better understanding of the significance of their role? Strengthening the connection between the mission and your board members will build their enthusiasm for elevating their commitment to performance.

Create a performance environment

To achieve and maintain a culture of performance, create an environment that encourages the behavior your organization is seeking.

Identify obstacles that may block your path to success and take action to eliminate them. Establish a method of measurement so everyone knows when expectations are being met. Peer pressure is a strong motivating influence, so once buy-in is achieved, encourage your board members to craft their own system of accountability. Instill a sense of pride in your organization's mission that inspires enthusiasm and performance. Work to develop positive team chemistry by creating and nurturing an atmosphere that helps board members feel united in their efforts to achieve a common goal. Model the behavior you want: Be obviously prepared for meetings, actively participate in board discussions with good ideas and questions, and personally meet engagement expectations. Celebrate every success so your board members can enjoy that priceless sense of accomplishment.

Recognize that change means altering behavior and that hesitation to embrace it is a common reaction. If it is time for your board to move to a higher level of engagement that will enable it to take on added responsibilities, implement these steps to build and sustain a high-performance environment.

To create transformation in your board performance culture, don't just declare that a change in culture will be happening. Follow a deliberate path that leads to the achievements you aspire to.

....

Develop your action steps

- How would you evaluate your board's performance culture?

- What are specific performance issues to address?

- What are identifiable causes of culture challenges?

- How can your board be engaged in making needed culture changes?

15

DEVELOP STRONG
BOARD LEADERSHIP

Too often, we need look no further than the leadership to see why a board isn't meeting performance expectations. It's a good place to start if you want to identify sources of frustration associated with a volunteer board.

Those in leadership roles are primary in determining whether or not the overall board member experience is one that influences in a positive way how individuals feel about their board service. Furthermore, the reputation of a board's leadership strongly influences board recruitment success.

Filling management positions requires planning well ahead. Organizations must first identify their leadership needs and then commit to corresponding standards of excellence. Doesn't it make sense that a purposeful process that considers qualified and willing board candidates would correlate to better leadership performance?

Let's look at two essential elements for developing strong board leadership—selection and preparation.

BE INTENTIONAL WITH LEADERSHIP SELECTION

I hear laughter, but it's not a good thing. It's the response I get every time I ask an audience about selecting leaders by the method of "whoever isn't in the room gets elected."

The question is not meant to be funny, so the consistent reaction makes a distressing point. This haphazard selection method is all too familiar to nonprofits, associations, and other groups with volunteer leaders.

Is volunteer leadership selection a joke? Can an organization with such a casual approach—choosing leaders without much forethought—really be serious about **Is volunteer leadership** achieving its stated purpose? Shouldn't **selection a joke?** leadership selection be intentional instead of accidental?

RECOGNIZE THE CHALLENGE

Beyond my own research, there is further solid statistical validation of the frequency of unintentional leadership selection and development across the nonprofit sector. Many reports stress the need for nonprofits to up their game.

BoardSource's 2017 edition of *Leading with Intent* survey found that a considerable number of board chairs lack critical skills in key performance influencing areas. It emphasizes, "When it comes to board culture, the importance of the board chair's leadership cannot be overstated." According to the report, "There is a clear link between the ability of the board to work as a collaborative team and the board chair's leadership."

Imagine the frustration felt by the significant percentage of the respondents reporting the inability of their board chair to resolve conflict, build consensus, and reach compromise. Moreover, the reality for a large portion of the survey participants is that their board chairs are not fostering an environment that builds trust among the board members, not establishing clear expectations of board service, and not encouraging the board members to frame and discuss strategic questions.

Ouch! How effective do you think those boards are? Do you think they are realizing their full potential? It just makes sense to avoid those leadership shortcomings whenever possible. You have to wonder why the individuals who generated poor performance ratings were chosen for leadership roles in the first place.

The need for improving leadership selection and development is also recognized in the 2017 *Stanford Survey on Leadership and Management in the Nonprofit Sector*. The report lists weak and inadequate board leadership as a top challenge to the effectiveness of nonprofits. It identifies the lack of leadership training and the lack of necessary skills and experience as key factors in ineffective leadership.

Weak, inadequate board leadership is a top challenge to the effectiveness of nonprofits.

These findings follow a 2015 Stanford project in collaboration with the Rock Center for Corporate Governance that reported, "The skills, resources, and experiences of directors are not sufficient to meet the needs of most nonprofit organizations."

Voices of Board Chairs, a 2016 study by the Alliance for Nonprofit Management was conducted by its Alliance Governance Affinity Group. Its purpose was to gather information from nonprofit board chairs on how they prepare for their leadership role. The study revealed "about half of the respondents indicated they did nothing specific to prepare to become a board chair." And when considering possible preparatory steps like first holding a different officer seat or chairing a board committee, few indicated taking an intentional route to being a board chair. Only 48 percent of the respondents reported that they had held the role of vice chair. The research team believes their findings should "encourage boards to place a greater emphasis on intentional board chair preparation and succession planning, as well as to strengthen board leadership."

Nonprofits would serve themselves well by heeding these findings and advice. They should establish selection procedures that match qualification criteria to their specific needs.

STRENGTHEN YOUR SELECTION PROCESS

Let's look at how to attract good fits. In order to draw positive, performance-minded leaders who have your desired qualifications and leadership abilities, adopt these three practices for leadership succession.

Identify your organization's goals. How does your organization define success? A clear focus on purpose clarifies what leadership types you need.

Develop a pool of potential leaders who are a fit for your organization. Identifying candidates for leadership roles should be an ongoing process. The pool can be a source for future officers, committee project chairs, and board members. This recommendation is reinforced by the *Leading with Intent* survey participants. When asked, "What are the three most important areas the board should address to improve its own performance?" they indicated development of a board leadership pipeline as one of the top actions needed.

Establish a job description, as well as performance expectations, for every position. Have an honest conversation with potential leaders about time commitments and responsibilities. Make sure each individual is comfortable with the task at hand and is satisfied that they can meet the obligations.

As I've said before, sometimes a no may be the best answer when someone is asked to take on a leadership role. Don't force the prospect into a yes and end up with a critical position filled by someone who really doesn't have what it takes to lead your board.

EMPHASIZE CRITERIA IN BOARD MEMBER SOLICITATION

Naturally, organizations want to attract the best possible board prospects, but wishing doesn't make it so. The recruitment process must be intentional. Where to start? Let's look at the well-structured approaches of three successful organizations.

When the National Speakers Association (NSA), the American Society of Association Executives (ASAE), and the Florida Society of Association Executives (FSAE) provide qualification criteria and performance expectations for leadership positions to their membership, they ask interested prospects to submit background information; the NSA also conducts individual interviews. All three give contact information for prospects who have questions, and they all initiate their solicitations well in advance of decision-making deadlines.

Establish and communicate selection criteria to get qualified board candidates.

Consider how these three organizations have structured their board nomination announcements. How does your board solicitation communication compare?

NATIONAL SPEAKERS ASSOCIATION CALL FOR BOARD NOMINATIONS

I am writing to you to seek your assistance in identifying those individuals whom you feel could make a valuable contribution in service as a member of the Board of Directors of the National Speakers Association (NSA) for the coming year and beyond.

This Call for Nominations is one of the most critical aspects of NSA since it has the potential to shape our Association for years to come. With the selection of a new CEO, it is also critical that we identify those individuals who can help move NSA forward to be its most vital, vibrant, and valuable to its members.

If you are interested or if you would like to nominate someone to serve on the NSA Board of Directors, please put forward your name or the name of a colleague. Now is the time to do so. The deadline for receipt of your nomination is November 10 by the end of the business day at 5:00 p.m. Pacific Standard Time.

When thinking of individuals to nominate, please remember the following duties as a member of the NSA Board of Directors:

- *Must attend a minimum of three (3) Board meetings per year.*

- *Must cover the cost of travel, hotel, and most meals for the Board meetings.*

- *Must commit to spending time in collaboration with other Directors, members, and industry experts, which may impact the ability to conduct business activities during those dates.*

For this Call for Nominations, the NSA Board of Directors and the NSA Board Nominations Committee are especially interested in those individuals who have demonstrated one (or more) of the following skill sets:

- *Leadership Ability*

- *Financial Acumen*

- *Strategic Thinking*

- *Strategic Planning*

- *Diverse Background Experience*

- *Prior Board Experience*

- *Profitable Speaking Business Model*

For those nominees who pass an initial screening, each will be asked to complete an online questionnaire and attend an in-person interview during the Winter Conference (being held in Baltimore, MD) on February 16–18. There will be up to five (5) positions to fill.

Please send your name or the name of those individuals you wish to nominate to XXXXX.

Also, please feel free to pass along this Call for Nominations to anyone within our Association who you feel would best support the spirit of NSA and would be a good fit for our Board.

Thank you for your attention to this request. If you have any questions, please feel free to contact us at XXXXX.

AMERICAN SOCIETY OF ASSOCIATION EXECUTIVES CALL TO FILL OFFICER AND BOARD VACANCIES

ASAE and ASAE Foundation's Board of Directors need you! Here is your chance to help lead the association dedicated to furthering the profession of association management. ASAE and ASAE Foundation are currently seeking the following association professionals and industry partners to serve in leadership positions:

Secretary-Treasurer (Industry Partners are not eligible to serve as Officers) and At-Large Directors (4); Industry Partner (1)

The benefits are many:

- *A significant role in advancing your profession.*

- *An opportunity to enhance the value of ASAE and ASAE Foundation to the association community.*

- *Access to up-to-date information about the challenges facing your profession.*

- *The chance to exchange ideas and perspectives with other volunteer leaders.*

ASAE and ASAE Foundation value and seek diverse leadership as defined by race, ethnicity, gender, religion, age, sexual orientation, nationality, disability, appearance, geographic location, professional level, etc. It seeks leaders from all types and sizes of eligible organizations. The Leadership Committee has identified a number of desired attributes that will be part of the selection process for new Board members:

- *Demonstrated leadership commitment and involvement with ASAE and ASAE Foundation and the nonprofit community. Examples include but are not limited to: service on an ASAE and ASAE Foundation committee, section council, commission, task force, and/or obtained the CAE credential.*

- *Recognized leader in the association community. Examples include but are not limited to: serving as the chair of an Allied Society, ASAE, and ASAE Foundation committee, section council, commission, task force, or philanthropic organization.*

- *Relevant expertise in the disciplines of organizational management. Examples include but are not limited to: branding, fundraising, component relations, finance, international, strategic alliances.*

- *Commitment to participate in 3–4 board meetings a year. ASAE board members are asked to provide financial support to Annual Giving, APAC, Power of A, special events and/or campaigns.*

- *Positive leadership attributes; emotional intelligence; ability to work collaboratively and engage in appropriate debate and discussion when needed.*

- *Visionary and strategic thinker. Demonstrated ability of new and innovative programs within their sphere of influence. Examples include, but are not limited to: incorporating strategy, leadership, future focus, risk taking, and an entrepreneur spirit.*

We want and need to hear from you. If you are interested in serving, or know of potential board members you would like to recommend, please contact XXXXX.

Nominations must be received no later than April 27.

FLORIDA SOCIETY OF ASSOCIATION EXECUTIVES (FSAE) CALL FOR BOARD NOMINATIONS

The FSAE and Foundation Nominating Committees are seeking nominations (Self-Nominations only) for Executive and Associate individuals with leadership experience to serve as Directors At-Large on the FSAE Board of Directors as well as Officers and Trustees for the Foundation Board of Trustees.

Members of the Board provide leadership, a shared vision and sense of mission and are responsible for the fiscal health of our organization. We are looking for leaders with:

- *Proven performance and a commitment to the organization*

- *Time and ability to serve*

- *Understanding of teamwork; communication and mentoring skills*

- *Sound judgment and integrity*

- *Enthusiasm and the ability to be a strategic, visionary thinker*

To apply, please review the criteria online and complete your nomination application by Friday, March 30.

All three organizations specify attributes or abilities they are looking for in candidates for their open seats. In addition, two specify criteria unique to their needs, one lists required skill sets, and the other lists the benefits of serving. All three organizations are purposeful in identifying their expectations; they are not winging it.

How does your organization communicate its opportunities for leadership nominations? How can you use these examples as models for improving your process?

PREPARE LEADERS FOR SUCCESS

Leadership selection by default will contribute to an environment that promotes frustration. It can also invite disaster. Don't assume that just because someone is elected to be chair, they will know what to do or will magically have the ability to do it successfully.

Here's a word of caution: Corporate-world success doesn't automatically translate into success in leading volunteers. Does your prospect have a history of positive, productive volunteer leadership that indicates they can adapt to asking rather than telling?

Those "willing to try" because no qualified candidates are available or aren't stepping forward are not recommended options. That is not to say well-meaning individuals with good intentions, though unprepared, don't have the potential to be successful. Just bear in mind how much time and on-the-job training your organization can afford.

Every organization is unique. What action is needed to ensure that your future leaders are prepared to lead?

Speaker Monica Wofford poses an on-point question. "What happens when someone gets promoted and they're not prepared for a leadership position?"

The answer: There are consequences—not necessarily good ones.

Here is my own painful story of taking on a task I wasn't prepared for.

What was I thinking?

It's hard to believe now that, at one time, I was a runner. I was able to earn a college scholarship to Jacksonville State University and competed in cross country and distance events during track season. At one point, I naively thought the idea of entering an event that most rational people would recognize to be a grueling challenge sounded like fun. Things would have gone better if I'd remembered the key lesson from my days as a Boy Scout: Be prepared.

I convinced teammate Thomas Odom to go along, and we enthusiastically submitted our entry forms for Atlanta's Peach Bowl Marathon. The fact that we had never trained for any distance remotely close to a marathon's 26.2 miles did not deter us. We were so confident we were up to the challenge that we made no adjustments to our regular training schedule. We were setting ourselves up for failure.

Well into the race, I still had delusions of completing the full distance, but my mind and body were only playing tricks on me. At the twenty-mile mark, with my body screaming that this had to be the dumbest thing I had ever attempted, I collapsed in a painful heap. It was failure accompanied by extreme pain. However, it was not a total loss. My ill-fated marathon experience has served as a lasting reminder of the necessity of laying the appropriate groundwork for facing a difficult challenge.

Organizations have the responsibility not to set their leaders up for failure. Likewise, individuals who want to answer the call to serve in a leadership position should take the time to fully investigate the role's requirements and whether they have work to do in order to meet them.

Avoid consequences like failure and pain. If the anticipated demands are somewhat beyond the level of experience or expertise of someone you are considering for a leadership role, be willing to acknowledge that reality. All parties must commit to the preparation needed to achieve success. Don't limit preparation to only the incoming chair or president. Make sure those in the leadership pipeline are appropriately groomed for new roles.

When looking at your prospect list, first consider whether they have the requisite skills and experience your organization needs. Although every organization is different and preferred leadership attributes will shift according to the current challenges and opportunities, there are basic skill sets that will always be relevant. A strong leader

- Has a positive leadership style that promotes consensus building and collaboration

- Has good communication skills

- Facilitates group conversation that engages all parties

- Delegates and follows up

- Pays attention to details

- Takes initiative

- Shares credit with others

- Models positive personality and behavior

- Commits extra time as needed

- Thinks strategically

- Has a vision for mission success

- Has a demonstrated donor history

Once you have found the right people for your positions, these additional actions will help set them up for leadership success:

- Take advantage of educational opportunities

- Send those in your pipeline to state or national conferences

- Consider using resources who specialize in volunteer leadership training

- Use events and activities as training tools so those with less organizational experience have opportunities to learn

- Invite future leaders to sit in on board or other key committee meetings

- Designate someone to serve as a mentor to those in your pool (which is also a great way to involve more experienced leaders)

A training path for prospects could include stepping up involvement, taking on increased responsibilities to gain greater understanding of how the organization functions, and self-study to acquire needed skills. Note: Individuals with leadership aspirations can be encouraged to take initiative to prepare themselves for the roles they seek. If a situation arises (and it often does) when someone is thrust unexpectedly into a leadership role, initiate catch-up actions to get them up to speed.

SELECT WITH INTENTION AND CONFIRM PREPARATION

The business of nonprofits is growing more complex. Strong effective board leadership is necessary to provide visionary, action-oriented guidance. If you want good, drama-free leaders, it's about selection and preparation.

Nonprofits can significantly reduce the frustration associated with boards by avoiding frustration-causing leadership-selection mistakes. Doesn't it make sense that a deliberate selection process that considers organizational criteria and individual qualification and that prepares future leaders would correlate with better leadership performance? Both the previously mentioned research and my own examination of board behavior say yes.

Pay attention to succession planning. Strengthen your selection process by preparing those being promoted to leadership roles to assume the responsibilities involved. Include development opportunities in the future-leader grooming process so they will gain the necessary skills and experience that nurtures their success. Make your board leadership intentional, not accidental.

....

Develop your action steps

- How can you improve your board selection process?

- What actions will help ensure that future leaders are better prepared?

- What board chair training should your organization provide?

- How can you help your board chair be a more effective leader?

16

BENEFIT FROM A COLLABORATIVE, INNOVATIVE, AND STRATEGIC-THINKING BOARD

A nonprofit board is a high-value asset. Organizations that don't keep this fact top-of-mind are wasting their board members' talents, skills, experiences, and passion to serve, as my survey demonstrates. Furthermore, board members have shared with me that when they don't have an opportunity to be involved in ways that take advantage of their personal and professional abilities, they feel much frustration.

Let me tell you about the consequences of one of the worst examples of a noncollaborative board that I have witnessed. The board leadership clearly stated there was no intention to involve other board members in decision-making. The chair pushed his personal agenda, and any disagreement was rejected. Meetings were dominated by never-ending personality clashes and constant arguments. The consequence of this highly dysfunctional situation was the board's attention being diverted from what mattered most—their significant financial challenges. After much frustration, valuable potential leadership resigned, and the organization lost the very people who could have saved it.

Now let's look at a collaborative board that stands in stark contrast. When a museum board realized that a major review of the museum's direction was in order, they brought me in to facilitate the critical conversation to set action priorities and to get clarification on board performance expectations. The board members worked together to identify their vision for the future and to determine what actions would be needed to get them where they wanted to be. By working collaboratively, they were able to establish board engagement standards for how they would move forward and support the staff in its role in implementing the master plan. The collaboration from the board's planning activity has continued, and the result is that the museum is positioned for success well into the future with its multimillion-dollar expansion.

When boards take a collaborative team approach, they far exceed the results they would otherwise achieve. An atmosphere of collaboration stimulates supportive participation and leverages individual strengths. It also unleashes problem-solving creativity. In addition, boards that are viewed as a resource for developing innovative solutions can make major contributions to current and future challenges. Organizations that encourage the board's vision are also better equipped to recognize and take advantage of worthwhile opportunities. Moreover, when board members participate in developing strategies, the board members have enthusiasm for implementing them. This is the support that leads organizations to meet and exceed their goals.

Organizations that don't take these concepts seriously are asking for double frustration: The organizations are frustrated when the board doesn't respond with commitment to taking action, and the board members are frustrated when they feel underused. Involving board members in critical conversations that help develop organizational focus and direction lets them know their opinions are valued. Doesn't it make sense to welcome these valuable resources to dialogue about major challenges and optimal direction?

Organizations are frustrated when the board doesn't respond with commitment to taking action, and board members are frustrated when they feel underused.

Think about the benefits of a board that functions at a maximum performance level. When you develop a board that works collaboratively, has a willingness to consider innovative approaches, and thinks and acts strategically, you transform it into an asset that provides both guidance and action that helps the organization adapt to meet new challenges. The transformative environment also serves as a motivational engagement tool for current and future board members.

BENEFIT FROM A COLLABORATIVE BOARD

"Nonprofits must collaborate or evaporate." This is a trademark saying of my friend and longtime United Way executive Ray Salazar. Ray is quick to point out he didn't coin the expression but has adopted it as a guiding belief. Despite the recognized benefits, putting Ray's words into practice can be easier said than done. For instance, whether being implemented within multiple locations of a single organization, between two or more groups, or within a group of individuals, successfully developing a culture of collaboration requires the understanding of what makes a cooperative effort work. And as with any good relationship, achieving positive results demands that the parties are fully committed to the process, which, at times, can be difficult.

Sometimes, geographic separation creates a physical obstacle between different service centers of the same agency. Distance can hinder board member relationships. When boards meet infrequently, in-person and personal connection may be difficult.

Another example is that working collaboratively can require overcoming past practices of either individual or organizational prejudice, including turf protection that discourages cooperation with others. Crossing the boundaries between departmental silos or competing agencies to achieve a common goal might make for a logical alliance but can be challenging to achieve.

I was called in as a consultant to resolve such a situation at a social service agency embroiled in a heated internal struggle between the administrative and service delivery components. A survey revealed they had totally different perspectives on how to achieve their organization's mission. Each considered its role more important and thought the other was operating in ways detrimental to the organization. Of course, both groups were vital, and taking steps to create a cooperative workplace was critical to resolving their performance-paralyzing conflict. Once they were brought together and realized their interdependence, the organization was able to meet and exceed its goals.

The benefits of collaboration among board members are practically unlimited for nonprofits seeking answers to challenges or ways to take advantage of new opportunities and initiatives. In addition, a board may benefit from strategic partnerships with other nonprofits.

A collaborative culture generates innovative solutions and incorporates this essential element: buy-in necessary for successfully implementing those new strategies. Whether resolving internal issues, launching a new initiative, or structuring a strategic alliance, collaborating is about breaking down barriers that hinder progress.

MAKE COLLABORATION WORK

The essence of collaboration is people interacting positively with one another to achieve a mutually desired result. Because the human element is the primary influence that must be taken into account, developing a new culture can involve behavior change and relationship building. Trust, understanding, appreciation, and sensitivity about feelings and egos are essential elements. There has to be mutual acceptance of personality differences and diverse ideas.

Courteous communication must be a priority; everyone must remember that listening is the secret sauce that makes communication work. This takes time, so carefully crafting an environment that nurtures new and respectful relationships is crucial.

Identify collaboration champions to lead the effort. Recognize and reward individuals modeling the behavior you want. Consider involving a facilitator to moderate conversations so they stay on track and remain positive.

To attract needed participation for solving an issue, Ray Salazar has found that telling a story with a compelling outcome gets attention. He says, "It should scream at the listener, so they react by responding, 'I didn't know that, but now I do, and I want to do something about it.'" He adds that the entire board should feel that they own the problem and that no one can accomplish needed results alone. This is vital to getting the structural pieces to work together.

Other characteristics of a successful collaborative effort also include the knowledge that you give up something to get more and that individuals accept roles within a team framework. While respect and decorum are required, spirited debate should actually be encouraged as a way of ensuring the best ideas come forward.

CREATE A PROCESS

The creative process that produced the hit movies *Toy Story*, *Finding Nemo*, and *Inside Out* offers lessons that can help nonprofits seeking to create collaborative relationships. Ed Catmull is a cofounder of Pixar Animation Studios and president of Pixar Animation and Disney Animation. In his book *Creativity, Inc.*, Catmull reveals that Pixar films are produced through the creative efforts of hundreds of moviemaking professionals. Many groups must work together to create a movie project that meets both Pixar's high standards and box office expectations.

According to Catmull, getting to a finished product revolves around idea sharing and joint problem solving. Catmull credits the company's success to teamwork that channels naturally occurring creative conflict in a positive direction.

He shares eight essential keys to building Pixar's successful culture of collaboration: First, establish a safe environment for exchange of ideas so that fear of failure or rejection is not an issue. Don't take the opinions of others as a personal attack, and conversely, don't make sharing an opinion a personal attack. Be willing to give up control; collaboration participants must accept input from others and be willing to let go of practices that don't work. Don't succumb to feelings of winning and losing; give-and-take interaction should produce balanced solutions. Be ready to listen and prepared to hear the truth and viewpoints that challenge the status quo. Know the difference between criticism and constructive criticism. One tears apart and the other builds. Don't be the one who can't differentiate. Welcome disagreement as an opportunity to test ideas so the best concepts survive. Finally, schedule progress reports for review and frank evaluation.

Also important to the Pixar process is the establishment of an oversight group to make certain that structural ground rules stay intact, and engagement stays on a positive course.

ACHIEVE TRANSFORMATIVE RESULTS

Imagine a board environment where everyone supports each other and is engaged in stimulating, idea-generating, and problem-solving conversation. Imagine the results when new ideas are both welcomed and encouraged, and individuals are not afraid to share out loud. Imagine the world of nonprofits where the best ideas come forward and are embraced so that you avoid duplication of services, you save on costs, you maximize funding, and you dramatically enhance outcomes.

Implementing all of these action steps for developing your collaboration process will indeed transform imagined outcomes into reality. By creating a culture of collaboration, a board puts the supportive structure in place for becoming an innovative and transformative board.

SEE COLLABORATION OF THE FUTURE—NOW

Jacob Morgan, author of *The Collaborative Organization*, says, "Technological innovations are enabling collaboration because they have changed how we communicate and share information with one another."

He believes that these communication platforms are creating a society that is more connected and collaborative than ever before. According to Morgan, "People are becoming accustomed to interacting and collaborating with one another through social and collaborative platforms and are bringing these habits and methods with them into the workplace."

Morgan's assessment indicates this technology-inspired evolution can lead to a more naturally collaborative society.

BENEFIT FROM AN INNOVATIVE BOARD

Developing a board engaged in innovative thinking can help you realize multiple benefits. The organization is served by getting positive encouragement and support for finding new approaches to recurring challenges not currently being resolved. Innovation provides creative options for long-standing organizations whose performance is not as effective as perhaps it once was. In addition, innovation provides solutions for anticipated future challenges—and perhaps allows the organization to avoid some other issues altogether.

A board engaged in innovative thinking focuses on the power of possibility. Rather than the uninspiring, traditional, and limited board activity of approving minutes, listening to reports, and adjourning with board members feeling they have had little or no impact, board meetings are transformed into dynamic, imaginative, and inspired sessions.

An innovative board is energized and fun and will be much more motivated to set and meet high levels of performance expectations. Organizations that want the benefit of innovation and board leaders who want to develop an innovative board can start by gaining an understanding of how to make it work.

An innovative board is energized and fun and will be much more motivated to set and meet high levels of performance expectations.

MAKE INNOVATION WORK

Making innovation work means going beyond following generally accepted best practices just because that's what everyone else does. Being innovative means challenging current practices to determine whether or not they are indeed the best for your organization. If you feel your nonprofit is acting like a dog chasing its tail, constantly chasing elusive solutions, it may have fallen into a creative rut. It's time for a new direction.

Issues such as donor retention, volunteer turnover, and board member engagement are just a few of the persistent problems plaguing nonprofits. Staff and board members have attended training and conferences, and they are paying attention to what others are doing. They are making efforts to implement the recommended best practices that the nonprofit sector subscribes to. But the results you seek aren't coming. Why continue to do what doesn't work?

Perhaps best practices that don't produce positive outcomes aren't best after all. Speaker Stephen Shapiro is an expert on innovation. His book *Best Practices Are Stupid* examines why applying conventional solutions to conventional problems can be a barrier to success. Stephen's book provides action strategies for using innovative thinking to identify effective approaches to organizational issues.

He offers three reasons why best practices are stupid: Replication is not innovation; if you are copying others, you are playing a game of catch-up. What works for one organization may not work for another, because there may be no cultural or strategic fit. Practices we label as best may not even be the reason an organization has become successful.

Despite your best efforts, what results aren't happening for you? Are you stuck in neutral, unable to move forward? Being immersed in the day-to-day can cause creative blinders that block your path to success.

According to Stephen, fresh perspective often generates breakthrough solutions. New and unintended product applications (think about sticky notes) that completely revitalize a business and other answers to difficult problems can come from sources with no apparent connection to those struggling with a tough challenge. In addition, what's not being done can affect performance as much as continuing what isn't working.

The MacArthur Foundation is an example of funders changing their approach to funding charitable causes. They realized what they weren't doing had a significant influence on the effectiveness of their efforts. In the past, the foundation provided financial support without regard to focused giving and without concern for measurable outcomes. That has changed with their shift to a concerted strategy for specific support targets and their desire to ensure maximum impact for their investments by adopting expectations for results.

Evaluate your practices to see if they are producing positive outcomes. If they're not, change them.

Another example of the trend toward rethinking past and current practices is BoardSource's publication *Gala Addiction*, which urges evaluation of fundraising events and consideration of adopting new approaches to the development of needed

Don't let conditioned behavior hold your cause back. Ask, "How can our nonprofit and board be unique?"

financial support. It takes commitment to a process that allows innovation to occur. Don't let conditioned behavior hold your cause back. Ask, "How can our nonprofit and board be unique?"

The way it's always been done can be a performance killer. Consider adopting practices that will make a transformative difference. Differentiate from others that provide a similar service, solicit from the same donor pool, or recruit the same volunteers and board members.

An innovative board seeks fresh perspective to identify possibilities for new direction. An innovative board exposes itself to new thinking that comes from greater diversity in board member composition. An innovative board adopts changes in its practices to allow for collaborative conversation that introduces new concepts, solicits different ideas, and recognizes board member contribution to innovative thought. Finally, an innovative board encourages the organization to undertake inspired practices and supports providing resources for enabling the organization to successfully achieve and maintain a culture of innovation.

Build on your board's creative culture by keeping it top of mind when recruiting. When evaluating board prospects, look for personality characteristics that are conducive to visionary thinking. Look for individuals who have demonstrated a willingness to work collaboratively with others and those who will make a positive contribution in an innovation focused environment.

When you encourage the development of an innovative board as a key strategy, you enhance both your organization's effectiveness and your board member engagement. Moreover, innovative boards working together in a spirit of collaboration can be a tremendous resource in the development of strategic action plans that surpass current vision.

QUESTIONS TO ACT ON

A board can initiate innovative action by answering these three questions:

- What current practices should we reconsider?
- What new practices could or should we adopt?
- Who or what resources can be a source of productive thinking for our nonprofit and board?

BENEFIT FROM A STRATEGIC-MINDED BOARD

Organizations that don't take advantage of board member participation in planning are compounding their self-inflicted pain. Sometimes, nonprofit leaders think they will save time and money and avoid the hassle of uncooperative board members, stakeholders, or staff by writing a plan themselves.

Big mistake.

Certainly, the do-it-yourselfers can write a plan, but then whose plan is it? As noted earlier, board members feel resentful when left out of the planning process. Furthermore, they are frustrated when organizations have no apparent strategic direction: A lack of focus is a natural by-product. Unfortunately, all of this is far too common.

The opposite challenge with boards and planning involvement is the difficulty in getting board members to accept opportunities to participate in planning activities such as planning retreats. In my experience, this reluctance is usually a consequence of past experiences that seemed to be a waste of time. When board members don't see their involvement in a planning exercise translating into a plan that actually gets implemented, it further reinforces to them that their time was wasted. It can be a downward spiral.

RECOGNIZE WHAT IS LOST BY FAILING TO PLAN

Although planning should be an essential activity for any organization, nonprofits often leave plans gathering dust on a shelf, or they do no planning at all. In my work, I often hear how little time nonprofit leaders devote to it. When I ask audiences of nonprofit leaders if they engage in strategic planning, have an annual action plan, or make time to plan out the projects and activities that are critical to their success, the all too frequent response is that they don't. I get plenty of reasons and excuses as to why not. One of the most frequent is "Everyone is just too busy."

Ironically, those same nonprofit professionals confirm that they are well aware of the benefits of dedicated planning: It creates structure and focus, identifies potential solutions to anticipated problems, saves time, and establishes measurable goals with strategies for achieving them. Planning also sets desired performance levels, which allow for evaluation and accountability. They acknowledge all of this. So, in failing to act, these nonprofits are wasting time, money, and human resources—by choice.

My own experience that planning is a missing tool in the nonprofit toolbox is confirmed by two significant reports.

The first, the Evelyn and Walter Hass Jr. Fund and Compass Point report *UnderDeveloped: A National Study of Challenges Facing Nonprofit Fundraising*, shares that more than 23 percent of nonprofits nationwide don't have plans for their fundraising efforts. Imagine, almost one quarter of the country's nonprofits are not planning for the financial lifeblood that enables them to achieve their all-important missions! Worse yet, if an organization doesn't plan how to get necessary financial support, isn't it likely that it isn't strategizing for many of its other important activities?

The second significant report, BoardSource's *Leading with Intent: A National Index of Nonprofit Board Practices 2015*, points out further deficiencies in planning. According to survey findings, strategic planning remains among the top five areas needing board improvement. Furthermore, the report includes this strong, grim assessment of those failing to do their due diligence: "Organizations that do not have a formal written strategic plan or have not revised it within the past five years do a disservice to their mission, constituents, and boards." The need for planning and strategic engagement by boards was further reinforced in the 2021 edition of *Leading with Intent*.

If your organization is one of those that's too busy to plan, you are winging it. You shouldn't be surprised at your inability to reach your goals. Failure to plan has a direct impact on board—and organization—performance.

IMPROVE BOARD PLANNING
SESSION PARTICIPATION

Unfortunately, many organizations tolerate low attendance by those who should be present, a problem that increases when volunteers are involved. *Leading with Intent* makes this telling observation: "While 81 percent of boards approve the final strategic plan, only 20 percent of CEOs give their boards an A for effort in adopting and following it."

Individual buy-in does not arise from merely voting to approve a plan that the individual has no involvement in developing. Without foundational participation in decision-making, implementation of the plan goes nowhere.

Consider an approach of inclusion. Take these steps:

1. Use planning as an engagement tool

2. Get needed participation by making development of your planning team a project

3. Carefully recruit and reward participants

4. Show them the benefits your new or revised plan could have

5. Build enthusiasm that creates ownership

Then exercise patience. Allow the team to identify the goals, objectives, and needed action steps that they actually have a passion for. Dr. Jack Hawkins, chancellor of Troy University, shared this piece of wisdom with me: "If they help bake the cake, they own the cake."

"If they help bake the cake, they own the cake."

It may be a challenge in the short term, but in the long term, engaged planners will be much more willing to accept and follow through on implementation tasks.

If you struggle with board participation challenges for

planning activities, I have nine tips to make your planning sessions successful:

Involve board members in organizing the planning session

Those involved will generate their own creative ideas for an effective session, and their advance participation produces buy-in for the process and support for the plans the session produces. This expanded involvement also makes an exercise out of planning the planning session, which itself generates enthusiasm and greatly increases the degree of success you will enjoy.

Don't repeat mistakes of the past

There are reasons that previous attempts to secure participation have not been successful. Take time to understand why and be honest with your assessment. Seek out opinions from past participants and from those who should have been attending but didn't and use that feedback to make needed corrections. Here are some questions to ask yourself for more clarification:

- Could past sessions be seen as a waste of time?

- Were potential participants given appropriate notice?

- Was the planning activity planned, organized, and conducted with a sense of purpose?

- Was time allocated used effectively and efficiently?

- Was discussion dominated by a single person or just a few individuals?

- Were opinions elicited from those who were present but quiet?

- Are those who may have different or opposing viewpoints made to feel their opinions are welcomed?

- Did participants leave with a sense of accomplishment?

- Were participants recognized for their contributions to the organization's planning efforts?

- Was follow-up action taken on strategies that were developed?

Set participation goals

Identify who should be present if your session is to be a success. If your ideal attendees are volunteer board members, set a percentage goal of the board who must be present, and make every effort possible to meet it.

Communicate individually to let people know how much your organization needs their participation and how much you value their insight. Ask for a personal commitment for attendance. Don't accept "will try," "plan to," or "should be able to" as solid answers. You should know exactly who will attend prior to your activity. Understand that if you can't confirm attendance in advance, the chances are good that you won't reach your participation goals. Send out reminders to help ensure attendance. If someone who wants to participate cannot be present, consider a phone-in or video option.

Reaffirm the significance of participation with personal messages from the organization's top leader. If your session involves volunteers, it's a nice ego stroke. If it involves staff, it's hard to turn down the boss!

Avoid schedule conflicts

Schedule the planning activity far enough in advance to avoid potential scheduling conflicts. It may sound like common sense, but sometimes the organization already has other planned activities, important deadlines, or a heavy vacation season. Obtain schedule availability from the desired participants and set your date when most people can make it. Even better, set your activity on a regular, recurring schedule.

If someone would like to participate but cannot attend the session, phone in, or attend virtually, consider asking that person to submit in advance ideas and suggestions that can be shared with the rest of the planning team.

Establish expected outcomes

Have a specific purpose for your session. Communicate the intended result in advance. (For example, create three new strategies for recruiting volunteers or members.) Your participants will be able to arrive with ideas already formulated. Identifying an expected outcome will also help keep the session focused on the primary task at hand and be more efficient.

Make sure the participants are prepared

Your planning team should know exactly what is expected of them. It's difficult to offer a qualified opinion when given a thick folder of financials, project proposals, and operational details without the opportunity to review materials prior to the time of the discussion. Help them be prepared by giving them information in advance.

Determine what format works best for your group

Take into account the personalities involved in your planning session. Use a meeting format that gets desired results and creates a positive experience that motivates people to participate in future sessions. Some food for thought:

- Do you need team building or fun activities?

- Will your team react more favorably to a strictly all-business session?

- What is the most productive length of time?

- Will you get best results by getting away from the office and working in a retreat setting, or will a few hours in an office conference room be more productive?

Have a designated facilitator

Having someone with the ability to get everyone engaged and keep the process moving and focused is critical for creating the successful planning session you need. Judge whether someone outside your organization is needed. An outside facilitator is often more effective at challenging, encouraging, drawing out opinions, and controlling discussion so it stays on a positive, productive track.

Advance preparation time with your facilitator is important.

The facilitator should do the necessary homework to be knowledgeable about the organization, be familiar with the backgrounds of the participants, and know the ideal outcome. A predetermined structure will maximize the activity.

Don't forget your post-event follow-up

Send personal thank you notes that mention specific contributions participants made and solicit feedback for future sessions from them. Send out a summary of the planning session, along with a copy of any final documents produced there. Give regular progress reports on implementing the plans the participants developed.

Achieving significant board participation in your organization's planning sessions inspires the buy-in for implementing the action items produced there. Create within your organization the realization of the vital importance of planning activities.

If you execute these action items, you are more likely to enjoy

- A higher level of preparation, participation, and enthusiasm in your planning sessions

- Continued enthusiasm for post-planning implementation

- Increased likelihood that your plans will move from languishing on dusty shelves to propelling you to mission success

Capitalize on diverse board member experience, talents, creative ideas, and personalities to build a collaborative, innovative, and strategic-thinking board. Doing so will empower your board to realize its potential as a high-value, visionary asset. Developing a board that functions at this level will also greatly contribute to ending your frustration with board performance and to elevating your board members' engagement.

....

Develop your action steps

- How can your nonprofit benefit from a collaborative, innovative, and strategic-thinking board?

- How can your board establish a collaborative culture?

- What actions are needed to encourage the sharing of innovative ideas?

- How can you use planning activity to stimulate board engagement?

17

CORRECT BOARD MEMBER (MIS)BEHAVIOR THAT AFFECTS GOVERNANCE

Sometimes boards or their individual members can get off track. The board performance issues brought forward in this book link directly to the governance role of boards and the actions that ensure that their oversight obligations are properly executed. When any combination of these problem circumstances exists, boards are not able to function as they should and their ability to govern as required is compromised.

Even more significant than simple frustration felt by board members is this: If these (mis)behaviors are not corrected, the organization puts itself at risk and the consequences can be devastating. Unfortunately, board member transgressions are a reality, and there are cases when maintaining accountability requires disciplinary action. Please note that we are not addressing legal or conflict of interest misbehaviors but, rather, those related to not meeting engagement expectations and improperly crossing the line between board and staff division of responsibilities.

Following the advice shared in this book will help your organization avoid the circumstances we are addressing. Preventative action is so much easier than a reactive response. As the maxim cautions, an ounce of prevention is worth a pound of cure.

Three specific performance issues are behavioral red flags:

- Failing to follow proper governance practices

- Showing no intention of meeting obligations

- Overstepping boundaries of a board member's role

If not dealt with, these situations will lead to a fractured relationship between staff and the board, foster frustration among individual board members, and create a dysfunctional board whose behavior will endanger the organization's mission.

IDENTIFY BOARD GOVERNANCE PERFORMANCE ISSUES

For insight about board performance and how it impacts governance, I reached out to Simone Joyaux. Simone's philosophy and her approach for recruiting board members and establishing standards of performance expectation are detailed in her book *Firing Lousy Board Members and Helping the Others Succeed.* It is a must-read for anyone dealing with volunteer board members.

To say Simone is passionate about fixing problems related to nonprofit board governance is an understatement. Anyone who has heard her speak, read her books, or followed her newsletter and social media posts can bear witness: She holds no punches. Interviewing this respected nonprofit thought leader was a treat.

Simone believes that good governance is critical for achieving a nonprofit's mission. She believes that many good causes suffer from "governance poorly done." According to Simone, misunderstanding both governance and its significance is the reason that many nonprofits fail to properly execute this vital responsibility.

Governance, in fact, is much more than just fundraising. Simone asserts that "governance is a collective activity," with the organization choosing board members who are both aware of this shared responsibility and capable of meeting it. As stewards representing a nonprofit's community of beneficiaries and supporters, board members must accept their responsibility for its oversight and guidance. Achieving this engagement requires an organization's leadership to have positive relationships with its board members and to communicate effectively with them. Naturally, the board's creativity in addressing challenges should be cultivated.

> **Governance, in fact, is much more than just fundraising. Board members must accept their responsibility for oversight and guidance.**

As Simone stresses, ignoring issues facing an organization is not good governance. Here are five of her suggestions for fixing board governance flaws:

- Get the right people as board members through better recruitment vetting

- Create performance expectations for board members

- Empower boards to perform by creating a culture of performance

- Don't confuse positive challenge with disruption

- Address governance-related issues

FEEL LIKE FIRING BOARD MEMBERS?

Nonprofit and association leaders experiencing frustration with board member performance will especially benefit from Simone's process for dealing with individuals who need to be "thanked and released."

Simone says she wrote her compelling book because "the health of the organization matters most, so firing bad performers is both acceptable and necessary." For those contemplating such an extreme action, it sounds like she's giving permission to proceed, right? However, before handing out pink slips at your next board meeting, she cautions, there are conditions that should be met first. These conditions are about developing a process that makes firing the last resort.

Despite the title, Simone initially focuses on preventing the need for firing by helping keep performance issues from arising. She characterizes *Firing Lousy Board Members* as a manual. The guidance it provides also helps resolve problems so board members worth keeping can be saved.

Termination is the appropriate alternative only if all else fails. A sampling of the key points critical to her process advises organizations to

- Acknowledge that there is shared responsibility for board member performance

- Examine organizational practices that may be contributing to unsatisfactory performance

- Not take challenges such as someone's status in the community or as a significant donor as an excuse for not addressing performance issues

- Establish a board composition process and reinforce it as a formalized policy

While Simone is not an advocate of wholesale dismissal of board members, she does believe boards should function as intended. If poor individual performance is the reason that's not the case, she emphasizes, "The mission is not being served by allowing nonperformers to stay." Articulating and applying her recommended action steps gives the person responsible for dealing with board member dismissal the opportunity to do so in an appropriate and professional manner.

STOP MEDDLING BOARD MEMBERS

Are nonprofit board members who cross the line of responsibility a problem or a symptom? I suggest that improperly aggressive board members are a symptom. This issue occurs because of the lack of an effective process for both recruiting and orientation, which are interrelated problems.

Incorporating screening, giving consideration to personality characteristics, researching the potential board members' history of involvement with other organizations, speaking with references, and conducting personal interviews with prospects should all be essential elements in board recruitment.

Properly vetting board candidates up front to determine whether they will be a good fit will help prevent involvement issues later. The series of *Leading with Intent* surveys from BoardSource continue to report that nonprofit executives are critical of board members who lack knowledge of their roles and responsibilities.

Should it be a surprise then when less than fully knowledgeable board members act in ways that are considered unacceptable?

Who is responsible for ensuring a board is properly educated in board procedure? Experience has shown me that many organizations don't give their board member orientation the attention this vital activity deserves. Approaches like one session and done or, even worse, "Here's the manual, and let us know if you have any questions" can't realistically be considered adequate, can they?

Consider using an orientation process that begins with prospective board members' initial contact and doesn't end until their involvement on the board is concluded. Ongoing orientation as part of a board's continuing education allows for reinforcement of important "thou shalt not do that" messages.

Prevent the occurrence of nonprofit or association board members inappropriately crossing the line of their responsibilities by evaluating your process for recruitment, orientation, and ongoing training. Change current recruitment practices that don't identify potential problem-causing board members in advance.

If your board members aren't sufficiently knowledgeable on their roles and responsibilities, consider how your current educational practices can be improved. Avoid meddling and other improper board behaviors by preventing the problems that cause these symptoms before they begin.

Governance is the priority responsibility of a nonprofit board. Sometimes an individual board member or the board itself will cross the line of what is considered proper behavior and is in conflict with their oversight duties. Many of the circumstances that trigger objectionable behavior can be avoided by taking action on the practices suggested throughout this book. Doesn't it make sense to be proactive in removing potential problem-causing situations?

Whether an intentional act or one of omission, actions that compromise governance must be corrected. The consequences of not doing so can jeopardize an organization's ability to achieve its desired success.

....

Develop your action plan

- How would you rate your board's understanding of its role and responsibilities?

- How would you rate the orientation and training you provide to new board members?

- How can your orientation and training be improved?

- What corrective action is needed to ensure proper governance behavior?

18

ENSURE FUTURE SUCCESS

If you are frustration-free with your board and all is going well with your board member relationships, congratulations! However, ensuring that your success continues can be a challenge. Take the time to apply the recommendations in this book. They cannot only help sustain the level of productivity your organization presently enjoys; they can also elevate it beyond what you were hoping for. When good practices (and best practices) become the norm, they will no longer be difficult.

KEEP YOUR EYE ON THE BASICS

As a sports fan, I am intrigued by the many elements teams employ to achieve success. Leadership, recruiting, structure, training, and discipline are just a few of the fundamentals necessary for reaching championship level. When teams at the top begin to slip, the reason is invariably that they lost sight of what got them there in the first place. It's time to refocus.

If nonprofits want to sustain their success, they also must pay attention to basics such as communication, orientation, planning, and evaluation. Challenge your organization to focus on these essentials. For example, what level of orientation and training do new board members and volunteers in your organization receive? Are they given a manual to read, an in-person session, or both? Which is the most effective for you?

Small things—perhaps seemingly insignificant things—can be big difference makers, as anyone in a long-term relationship knows. Don't let complacency allow you to take your eye off the basics that keep good board relationships intact. It's easier to maintain quality than it is to regain it, but it is never too late to improve.

Don't let complacency allow you to take your eye off the basics.

CHALLENGE THE STATUS QUO

No matter how good the status quo seems, clinging to today means being left behind tomorrow. Consistently challenge yourself to find ways to improve board relationships. If you are willing to do the necessary work to keep them fresh, you will avoid future problems before they become headaches or threats. It's what flourishing companies do, and it's what got them there—and what they continue to do.

ARE YOU DUE FOR A MAKEOVER?

As a grocery shopper, I have always enjoyed good customer experience at Publix. When it announced its initiative to rebuild existing stores, Publix triggered my curiosity. After all, business is great, and their stores are well maintained. Why would a company undertake such a major investment without a readily apparent reason?

Spokesman Dwaine Stevens helped me understand the company's philosophy. "We embrace and perpetuate a culture of providing an environment that creates an extraordinary shopping experience for our customers on each and every visit. A healthy and inviting facility enhances the shopping environment. Investments in people and real estate take priority in setting a 'point of difference' in the competitive landscape."

In other words, Publix isn't standing still. They are constantly looking for ways to improve.

Are your organization and board members constantly looking for ways to improve? Here is a six-question points of difference checklist to stimulate your thinking:

- Regardless of how well your organization is doing today, what action is needed to prepare your board for tomorrow?

- How long has it been since you have engaged in the process to update your strategic plan?

- Does board member involvement with fundraising need a fresh approach?

- Is your board engaged in developing big-picture solutions to big-picture challenges?

- Are you preparing for how your board will be affected by the dramatic generational shift now occurring?

- Is your board meeting performance expectations? If so, how are you ensuring that desired results continue? If not, what corrective steps can you take?

Publix offers an example of long-term thinking in action. Successful businesses don't sit on their success. The same is true of successful nonprofits and their boards. If you sense potential problems beginning to surface, take corrective action immediately.

DON'T EXPECT PROBLEMS TO FIX THEMSELVES

Before the start of each NASCAR race, drivers and their crew chiefs attend a pre-event safety briefing. They are reminded, "Problems with your car don't fix themselves." Race teams are advised that malfunctions such as loose wheels or mechanical failures need to be tended to and that "drivers should not stay out on the track and risk wrecking themselves or someone else."

What is the looming boardroom problem that your nonprofit or association needs to face in order to avoid a big wreck? Regardless of how large or small a challenge is, delaying action only makes the situation worse.

Here are five actions for addressing an issue your organization may be facing: Recognize that you have a problem and develop leadership buy-in for dealing with it. While that may sound like a no-brainer, many organizations are not willing to take on a tough challenge, and through their inaction they are choosing to ignore what could come back to bite them. For example, relationship issues that are allowed to fester are difficult to fix. Take small steps toward the solution, as brothers Chip and Dan Heath advise. Sometimes, a problem can be so big that resolution seems unachievable. The incremental approach creates a cumulative effect that leads to the solution. Identify options and get support for decisions. Commit the time and resources necessary for the correction process and make it a priority. Consider the best outside resources. Take action and communicate the results to those parties that have an interest in seeing your organization succeed. Just as in NASCAR competitions, your problems won't fix themselves. Don't put off correcting what may keep you from achieving your all-important mission.

Be aware that issues that are not readily apparent could be contributing to frustration experienced by both your organization and your board members. Sometimes, it's what you don't see that disrupts performance. When the board isn't functioning as it should, neither is the organization. Take the time to identify the specific problem, and don't make assumptions about what it couldn't possibly be.

DON'T WAIT FOR AN ORGANIZATIONAL HEART ATTACK

The symptoms of my health scare were low energy and high fatigue. The cause was a 99 percent blockage in my coronary artery—which is called the widow maker. The correction was a stent. The results were amazing.

My cardiologist informed me that the situation had taken most of a lifetime to develop. So, for years—perhaps decades—my body had been struggling because the critical blood flow that the heart is supposed to provide was steadily diminishing. I am now happily realizing the profound difference of having a heart that is actually functioning at 100 percent. Increased energy, productivity, and sharper mental focus are the surprising and welcomed benefits.

I couldn't help but see the parallel between a heart's relationship with the body and a board's relationship with the nonprofit it sustains. Similar to the heart's responsibility to supply blood and oxygen to the body, the board's responsibility is to provide the direction and energy that help the nonprofit to function at maximum potential.

There are likely many factors to a board's not functioning at 100 percent. In order to diagnose issues obstructing your board's performance, differentiate between symptom and cause. Only then can you identify the correction and the cure. For instance, a symptom could be a board's lack of fundraising, and the cause could be a failure to recruit the right board members. The correction should start with conversations with board members that help identify the cures that move the board to the results: optimum performance. Then you, too, can realize the profound difference of having a board that is actually performing at 100 percent.

Before my heart attack forced me to confront my symptoms, cause, correction, and cure, I was performing but not at my full potential. Likewise, if your board isn't confronting and processing your problems, your organization isn't performing at its full potential. And even if your organization is currently enjoying positive and productive relationships with and among your board members, nothing lasts forever. Clinging to today does indeed mean being left behind tomorrow. What problems are lying in wait for you, perhaps under your radar?

Whether current or future, frustrations with your board are very real impediments to full organization health: They will keep your board and your organization from being 100 percent engaged and performing at your potential.

Be candid. What complications are blocking your board from functioning as it should? What are the actual causes? What are realistic corrections and cures? When you answer these questions and take focused action, you will ensure your organization's success.

....

Develop your action steps

- What is your board's vision for future success?

- What actions are needed to ensure that success?

- What current board practices need to be done differently?

- What priority actions will you take after reading this book?

CONCLUSION

The frustration associated with nonprofit boards is real. For many, many organizations, relationships with their board members are a dysfunctional mess. And complaints go in both directions. Organizations charge that board members don't meet performance expectations. Board members participating in my research charge that organization staffs don't hold up their end in facilitating the proper functioning of the board.

When relationships between staff and board—and those among board members themselves—aren't operating in a positive and productive manner, the mission suffers. Much of the blame rests on the repeating cycle of poor practices that are in desperate need of change. You know Einstein's famous quote about doing things the same way and expecting a different result. Well, isn't it about time to consider something new to build positive non-profit organization relationships so that their performance has the opportunity to meet desired expectations?

Actually, it's long past time. So that became my goal: to find something new—something to transform the relation-ships between nonprofits and their board members. I wanted to end the frustrations on both sides and enable all parties to come together to build the collaborative culture necessary to achieve mission potential. This book became the platform to make the goal a reality.

Let's recap what we have discussed.

First, my survey of blue-chip nonprofit board members from across the country yielded illuminating responses. With the benefit of the board member perspective—one that is not considered often enough—I identified the most significant issues and their causes that contribute to board members not performing as expected. By combining suggestions from these board members with insights from colleagues who are recognized subject matter experts and solutions developed through my own experiences, I have crafted practical, easy-to-implement actions that can make the difference in eliminating board-associated problems in your organization.

Second, in order to realize their potential, organizations must have the right people on their boards. Everything is built on this foundation. Recruit them methodically.

Third, staff and board members must pay attention to the quality of the time board members spend with your organization. They are individuals. Know them: Know their backgrounds. Know their perspectives. Create a positive board experience for them.

Finally, the continuing success of your organization means anticipating inevitable changes and challenges and meeting them with forward thinking and pragmatic leadership.

Your organization might currently enjoy a highly effective and very engaged board; however, you can still profit from the lessons this book provides to help ensure that those positive, productive relationships remain strong.

The painful experience of COVID-19 that began in 2020 taught us that we can adjust to change better than we thought possible. It demonstrated that organizations must have in place leadership with the ability to lead and to set the example of adaptive behavior necessary to meet difficult demands. Leaders with the foresight to find new and creative paths to overcome adversity are the ones who will give their causes opportunity for long-term survival.

Remember this often-overlooked fact: Change represents opportunity. Wisely chosen, happy, and visionary board members will help your organization recognize and champion opportunities of value. A nonprofit organization's board is a high-value asset. Support and nurture yours and reap the rewards: You will avoid board frustration and dysfunction, and you will position yourself to face the future strategically and successfully.

ACKNOWLEDGMENTS

What a journey this book project has been!

Anyone who has authored a book knows the process is full of challenges. The roller coaster of ups and downs plays emotional tricks that can either provide needed inspiration or derail the project altogether. Many people have helped me stay on track. They and many others have played valuable roles in the writing of this book, and I am very grateful to all of them.

You might think that achieving publication success despite having to overcome years of difficult obstacles is deserving of self-congratulation. To be sure I am proud of this accomplishment; however, there are many others deserving of a place on the victory podium with me.

I am lucky to have had a broad variety of life experiences and relationships that have directly influenced this project. The list of individuals who have been a part of my life journey would read like the lengthy credits at the end of a movie.

Thank you to my family, friends, and community supporters in my hometown of Talladega, Alabama. They have had a warm, colorful, and lasting influence on me.

Thank you to many special people along the way, like those in the Jaycees, the world of NASCAR racing, and the National Speakers Association. They have afforded me the opportunities that developed my speaking, consulting, and writing skills, which now benefit the organizations I work with.

Thank you to the mentors who have shared their wisdom with me. They were willing to invest time and give advice that have shaped my life's path and the direction this book has taken.

Thank you to the individuals who participated in the original survey that became the foundation for this book. Their insights triggered the recognition of the critical missing element in the conversation about board performance and board member engagement—the board member perspective.

Thank you to those who influenced this book but unfortunately passed before its publication. I will always be grateful for their contributions.

Thank you to many subject matter experts. They generously gave their time for interviews and strengthened the impact of this book.

Thank you to many other valued sources and respected authors. Their research data and content further enhanced many of the practical solutions offered here.

Thank you to the team at Greenleaf Book Group for their publishing expertise and dedication to producing this comprehensive resource for the nonprofit community.

Thank you to my team of beta readers for their willingness to provide honest feedback on needed improvements. I definitely got no ego stroking or sugarcoating from Barry Banther, Nick Craw, Simone Joyaux, Gina Morgan, David Smith, Alyce Lee Stansbury, and Monica Wofford.

Thank you to the individuals who graciously provided endorsements. The support of these nonprofit hall of famers validates the many messages in this book.

Thank you to Bob Harris who wrote the foreword. He is an icon in the world of nonprofits, associations, and chambers of commerce.

Thank you to my wonderful network of friends and colleagues. Their encouragement, challenges when needed, and gentle nudges of "Are you finished yet?" helped me to indeed finish.

Thank you to my most amazing editor Denise McCabe. Credit goes to her for getting this book across the publication finish line in a form that anyone would be willing to read. Her superb editing skills, patience, guidance, encouragement, and friendship have helped produce a quality work.

Thank you to my mother and sisters. They have given me their ongoing enthusiasm.

Thank you to David, Tiffany, and grandson, Troy. They have been constant sources of support and inspiration.

My biggest thank you goes to my wife, Debbie. She has believed in this project from the beginning. Without her encouragement throughout the entire process, this book would not have been possible.

ABOUT THE AUTHOR

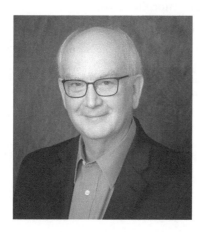

HARDY SMITH is a consultant and speaker who works with leaders who want to stop frustration with their volunteer boards. Through board retreats, workshops, keynotes, and planning sessions, Hardy provides solutions to board engagement challenges.

Hardy's extensive experience with diverse organizations provides the basis for his comprehensive book *Stop the Nonprofit Board Blame Game*. His results-oriented approach and ability to solve complex problems were developed during his longtime career in the high-performance world of NASCAR racing. That experience included strategic planning for some of the country's largest sports and entertainment facilities and spectator events.

Hardy has also had more than a decade of senior leadership

experience in local government, which further refined his skills in improving organizational performance. Hardy has wide-ranging personal and professional involvement with nonprofits, associations, chambers of commerce, and community groups nationwide. He has held numerous local, state, and national volunteer leadership positions that have further contributed to his in-depth understanding of nonprofit needs.

Hardy is a member of the National Speakers Association, Association of Fundraising Professionals, BoardSource, Florida Society of Association Executives, ASAE, and Association of Chamber of Commerce Executives. Hardy is also a faculty member of the U.S. Chamber of Commerce's Institute for Organization Management.

Learn more about Hardy by visiting his website:

www.hardysmith.com